INDIA THE MOTHER

INDIA THE MOTHER

Tapas Kumar Mukherjee

KALPAZ

ISBN : 978-93-5128-004-0

Price : ₹ 595

First Published 2014

Published by

Kalpaz Publications
C-30, Satyawati Nagar
Delhi-110052
Ph.: 9212142040
E-mail: kalpaz@hotmail.com

Laser Typesetting: Rudra Computer Graphics, Delhi
Printed at: G. Print Process, Delhi

Cataloging in Publication Data--DK
Courtesy: D.K. Agencies (P) Ltd. <docinfo@dkagencies.com>

India the mother / Tapas Kumar Mukherjee.
p. cm.
Includes index.
ISBN 9789351280040

1. Hinduism--Doctrines. 2. Spiritual life--Hinduism. 3. Vedanta. 4. Hindu philosophy. 5. Yoga. I. Mukherjee, Tapas Kumar.

DDC 294.52 23

Contents

Foreword

India from the time immemorial, destined to be a 'punya bhumi', 'the land of Karma', i.e., 'to be the land to which all souls on earth must come to account for Karma, the land to which every soul that is wending its way Godward must come to attain its last home, the land where humanity has attained its highest towards gentleness, towards generosity, towards purity, towards calmness, above all, the land of introspection and of spirituality'. And again, "this is the land, from whence, like the tidal waves, spirituality and philosophy have again and again rushed out and deluged the world, and this is the land from whence once more such tides must proceed in order to bring life and vigour into the decaying races of mankind". Thus, the element of the historical tradition of the territorial past, i.e., the geography wher the Himalayas are shaping the contours of history plays a vital role in determining Vivekananda's India. To him, the Himalayas stand for renunciation and "if these Himalayas are taken away from the history of religious India, there will be very little left behind". Another astonishing feature of Indian nationhood is its plurality emerged from the very nature India's geography and affirmed by her history. This pluralism almost without bounds in terms of religious, philosophical, ideological and political and so many others have co-existed in India in harmony since time immemorial. In Vivekananda's approximation. renunciation and service had been the two national ideals which turned out to be instrumental in reasserting the national life. He urged every Indians to intensify those two ideals in their personal as well as societal life with the aim of taking India to her greatest height once again.

It is a pleasure for all who use to look at India to be their actual mother that Sri Tapash Kumar Mukhopadhyay who happened to an ardent student in various diploma courses in the Ramakrishna Mission Vivekananda University at Belur Math, has ventured to bring out a compilation work consisting of the relevant portions from the complete works of Swami Vivekananda, Swami Abhedananda, Sister Nivedita and Sri Aurobindo. Undoubtedly, this compilation would inspire and motivate its readers to be intensely engaged in building up a glorified India in the years to come. I earnestly pray to the Almighty for the wide circulation of the thought provoking and invigorating words that the present publication contains.

Swami Tattwasarananda
Ramakrishna Mission
Sikshanamandira, Belur Math.

Preface

This is a compilation of selected portions from the complete works of different Great personalities, but interestingly we find in it not the difference among them, rather the concurrence only.

As a matter of fact, when I have gone through the complete works of Swami Vivekananda, Swami Abhedananda, Sister Nivedita and Sri Aurobindo, what appears to me the most striking one is their complete convergence of views about the role being played by India and her contribution from the time immemorial for the growth and upliftment of various civilizations of the world and for the whole mankind at large.

The point which has enthused me immensely to bring them in a common platform is that by doing so, we can get a resonance of thought they felt all alike that India has been the motherland of knowledge of each faculty of study and spiritual wisdom; later on other nations and races gathered the same from India alone.

I quote from the words of each of them, which shows how motherly role India has played all along :-

> "I am proud of belonging to a religion which has taught the world both tolerance and Universal acceptance. . . . . . . .I am proud of belonging to a Nation which has

sheltered the persecuted and refugees of all religions and all nations of the earth".

Swami Vivekananda
p.11, India the Mother

"The dawn of Aryan Civilization broke for the first time on the horizon not of Greece or Rome, not of Arabia or Persia, but of India, which may be called the motherland of metaphysics, philosophy, logic, astronomy, science, arts, music and medicine as well as of truly ethical religions".

Swami Abhedananda
p.89, India the Mother

"Before Europe was born, India has grasped the essential fact that the end of civilization lies in the making of men—not wealth, not power, not Organization."

Sister Nivedita
p.127, India the Mother

"This great and ancient nation was once the fountain of human light, the apex of human civilization, the exemplar of courage and humanity, the perfection of good Government and settled society, the mother of all religions, the teacher of all wisdom and philosophy."

Sri *Aurobindo*
p.133, India the Mother

We can see that the magnificent role India has played, when focused collectively, certainly have stronger appeal than that when it is focused by any single personality.

Therefore, I can very much aspire that this being a compilation from the works of four great personalities, will have a louder say to the people of India and people of the world, as regards knowing India in a better way.

Acknowledgements

I am grateful to my Acharya revered Swami ***Tattwasarananda Maharaj***, Principal, Ramkrishna Mission Sikshana Mandira, Belur Math, for his unerring guidance which has made me to proceed for publication of this work and it is really blessing to me that revered Swami Suparnananda Maharaj, Secretary, The Ramkrishna Mission Institute of Culture, Golpark, Kolkata has made such a highly encouraging remark on my writing on India. I pay my sincere regards to them.

Lastly, I express my deep sense of gratitude to all my beloved sisters, brothers and friends who have been instrumental in this work; and one name I can't help mention here is my elder sister Smt. Anita Bhattacharyya that without her inspiration and unflinching support this compilation work would not have been possible.

Synopsis

I have chosen the title "India the Mother" to reveal the truth that the God has made India the reservoir of all branches of knowledge and spiritual wisdom to cater it to the rest of the World.

India stands as the mother of all the races of the World, that she has accepted all with love and rejected none with hatred. She has acquired material knowledge and spiritual wisdom long, long before other races witnessed the light of civilisation, but India's generosity never ceased to scatter her acquired knowledge and wisdom to the rest of the World. To accelerate their pace of development in the process of evolution. All branches of knowledge, i.e., arts, science, literature, economics, philosophy, governance and whatsoever, has been originated in India and later on particularly Europe and some other parts of the World have made remarkable progress in science and technology, also in other branches of knowledge; but the most valuable contribution of India to the rest of the World is that the teaching she has imparted on the science of spirituality. The precious gift India could ever present to the humanity is her Vedanta philosophy. What does Vedanta teach us? It is oneness of the Universe. Vedanta tells us that all our misery comes through ignorance and this ignorance is the idea of manifoldness. So the separation between man and man, between nation and nation, between earth and moon between atom and atom are only apparent, truly there exists no separation but there exists absolute unity. Ultimately this Vedanta philosophy alone will enrich and glorify the human race and nothing else.

This book is a compilation work. I have collected portions from the complete works of Swami Vivekananda, Swami Abhedananda, Sister Nivedita and Sri Aurobindo, where each of them stressed the role of India to be a teacher to the rest of the World, as regards imparting education in all the branches of knowledge and at last on spirituality.

Let me quote from the words of Swami Vivekananda:

"Great indeed are the manifestation of muscular power and marvelous the manifestations of intellect expressing themselves through machines of science, yet none of these is more potent than the influence which spirit exerts upon the world."

India could only realize this fact and not Greece nor Rome nor any other race could realize the magnificence of the spirit and as such they concentrated towards the search for external nature and in contrast India inspite of being fully competent to excel in the search for external nature she concentrated in the search for inner nature.

From the words of Sri Aurobindo we could know that India had been the forerunner in all the branches of physical knowledge:

"...Not only was India in the first rank in mathematics astronomy, chemistry, medicine, surgery, all the branches of physical knowledge which were practiced in ancient times, but she was alongwith the greeks, the teacher of the Arabs from whom Europe recovered the lost habit of scientific enquiry and got the basis from which modern science started."

It is only recently i.e around nineteenth century or so, western countries have made remarkeable progress in the field of science and technology which has brought the economic prosperity in that region and they have become a recognised economic power indeed, among, other nations. Their standard of living though improved enormously but not the standard of life. Truly, they have made headway in technological advancement but alongwith it they welcome moral and spiritual bankruptcy, resulting in the decay of humanising force from within the human being. Thus man has become hungry like crocodile for money and power. This situation is certainly a threat to the human civilisation to flourish. This sort of negative development in the human society could not remain unnoticed by the eminent philosophers and thinkers worldwide. They have come to the conclusion that Indian spirituality can alone save the mankind from its downfall and bring peace in the World.

The great German Philosopher Schopenhouer says, "In the whole World there is no study so beneficial and so elevating as that of Upanishads. It has been solace of my life, it will be the solace of my death."

Sir Arnold Toynbee, the great historian speaking of our time (in the middle of twentieth century) in the history of mankind, held that "Today we are living in a transitional chapter of the World's history, but it is already becoming clear that a chapter which had a western beginning will have to have an Indian ending if it is not to end in the self destruction of the human race. Toynbee goes on to say that even these excellent utilitarian reasons, world peace and human survival are secondary reasons for following Indian wisdom. The primary reason is that it is true, it is rooted in a true vision of spiritual reality."

At the end of the synopsis on my chosen title "India The Mother" let me once again declare the fact in a nutshell that India has been generous to bestow her knowledge that she had acquired quite earlier to different races of the World and having cultivated they have excelled in the respective fields; but the last responsibility of India still remains unfulfilled that is to spiritualise the World. This task is the most difficult one because the people of the World will be able to enlighten themselves with the spiritual light (which is stored in India) only when their level of consciousness will be elevated at a certain standard; but whatsoever difficult the task may be, India is destined to accomplish her task by spiritualising the human race in the end. The real glory of humanity lies in achieving the enlightened state of mind but not in any other development in the material plane.

Dated: 17.7.2012 **Tapash Kumar Mukherjee**

1

Collection from the Complete Works of Swami Vivekananda

Sisters and Brothers of America,

It fills my heart with joy and I am unspeakable to rise in response to the warm and cordial welcome which you have given us. I thank you in the name of the most ancient order of monks in the world; and I thank you in the name of millions and millions of Hindu people of all classes and sections.

I thanks also to some of the speakers on this platform who, referring to the delegates from the Orient, have told you that these men from far-off nations may well claim the honour of bearing to different lands the idea of toleration. I am proud of belonging to a religion which has taught the world both tolerance and universal acceptance. We believe not only in universal toleration, but we accept all religions as true. I am proud of belonging to a nation which has sheltered the persecuted and the refugees of all religions and all nations of the earth. I am proud to tell you that we have gathered in our bosom the purest remnant of the Israelites, who came to Southern India and took refuge with us in the very year in which their holy temples were shattered to pieces by Roman tyranny. I am proud of belonging to the religion which has sheltered and is still fostering the remnant of the grand Zoroastrian nation. I will quote to you, brethren, a few lines from a hymn which I remember to have repeated from my earliest boyhood, which is every day repeated by millions of human beings: *"As the different streams having their sources in different places all mingle their water in the sea, so, O Lord, the different paths which men take through different tendencies, various though they appear, crooked or straight, all lead to Thee."*

The present convention, which is one of the most August assemblies ever held, is in itself a vindication, a declaration to the world of the wonderful doctrine preached in the Gita: *"Whoever comes to Me, through whatsever form, I reach him; all men are struggling through paths which in the end lead to me"*. Sectarianism, bigotry, and its horrible descendant, fanaticism, have long possessed this beautiful earth. They have filled the earth with violence, drenched it often and often with human blood, destroyed civilization and sent whole nations to despair. Had it not been for these horrible demons, human society would be far more advanced than it is now. But their time has come; and I fervently hope that the bell that tolled this morning in honour of this convention may be the death-knell of all fanaticism, of all persecutions with the sword or with the pen, and of all uncharitable feelings between persons wending their way to the same goal.

Three religions now stand in the world which have come down to us from time prehistoric - Hinduism, Zoroastrianism and Judaism. They have all received tremendous shocks and all of them prove by their survival and their internal strength. But while Judaism failed to absorb Christianity and was driven out of its place of birth by its all-conquering daughter, and a handful of Parsees is all that remains to tell the tale of their grand religion, sect after sect arose in India and seemed to shake the religion of the Vedas to its very foundations, but like the waters of the seashore in a tremendous earthquake it receded only for a while, only to return in an all-absorbing flood, a thousand times more vigorous, and when the tumult of the rush was over, these sects were all sucked in, absorbed, and assimilated into the immense body of the mother faith.

The Hindus have received their religion through revelation, the Vedas. They hold that the Vedas are without beginning and without end. It may sound ludicrous to this audience, how a book can be without beginning or end. But by the Vedas no books are meant. They mean the accumulated treasury of spiritual laws discovered by different persons in different times. Just as the law of gravitation existed before its discovery, and would exist if all humanity forgot it, so is it with the laws that govern the spiritual world. The moral, ethical, and spiritual relations between soul and soul and between individual spirits and the father of all spirits, were there before their discovery, and would remain even if we forgot them.

The discoverers of these laws are called Rishis, and we honour them as perfected beings. I am glad to tell this audience that some of the very greatest of them were women. Here it may be said that these laws as laws may be without end, but they must have had a beginning. The Vedas teach us that creation is without beginning or end. Science is said to have proved that the sum total of cosmic energy is always the same. Then, if there was a time when nothing existed, where was all this manifested energy? Some says it was in a potential form in God. In that case God is sometimes potential and sometimes kinetic, which would make him mutable. Everything mutable is a compound, and everything compound must undergo that change which is called destruction. So God would die, which is absurd. Therefore there never was a time when there was no creation.

Thus it is that the Vedas proclaim not a dreadful combination of unforgiving laws, not an endless prison of cause and effect, but that at the head of all these laws, in and through every particle of matter and force, stands one "by whose command the wind blows, the fire burns, the clouds rain, and death stalks upon the earth."

And what is His nature?

He is everywhere, the pure and formless one, the Almighty and the All-merciful, "Thou art our father, Thou art our mother, Thou art our beloved friend, Thou art the source of all strength; give us strength. Thou art He that beareth the burdens of the universe; help me bear the little burden of this life." Thus sang the Rishis of the Vedas. And how to worship Him? Through love. "He is to be worshipped as the one beloved, dearer than everything in this and the next life".

This is the doctrine of love declared in the Vedas, and let us see how it is fully developed and taught by Krishna, whom the Hindus believe to have been God incarnate on earth.

He taught that a man ought to live in this world like a lotus leaf, which grows in water but is never moistened by water; so a man ought to live in the world—his heart to God and his hands to work.

It is good to love God for hope of reward in this or the next world, but it is better to love God for love's sake, and the prayer goes: "Lord, I do not want wealth, neither children, nor learning. If it be Thy will, I shall go from birth to birth, but grant me this, that I may love Thee without the hope of reward—love unselfishlv for love's sake." One of the disciples of Krishna, the then Emperor of India, was driven from his kingdom by his enemies and had to take shelter with his queen in a forest in the Himalayas, and there one day the queen asked him. "How it was that he, the most virtuous of men, should suffer so much misery" Yudhishthira answered, "Behold, my queen, the Himalayas, how grand and beautiful they are; I love them. They do not give me anything, but my nature is to love the grand, the beautiful, therefore I love them. Similarly, I love the Lord. He is the source of all beauty, of all sublimity. He is the only object to be loved; my nature is to love Him, and therefore I love. I do not pray for anything; I do not ask for anything. Let Him place me wherever He likes. I must love Him for love's sake. I cannot trade in love."

...Therefore, to gain this infinite universal individuality, this miserable little prison-individuality must go. Then alone can death cease when I am one with life, then alone can misery cease when I am one with happiness itself, then alone can all errors cease when I am one with knowledge itself; and this is the necessary scientific conclusion. Science has proved to me that physical individuality is a delusion, that really my body is continuously changing in an unbroken ocean of matter; and Advaita (unity) is the necessary conclusion with my other counterpart, soul.

Science is nothing but the finding of unity. As soon as science would reach perfect unity, it would stop from further progress, because it would reach the goal. Thus Chemistry could not progress farther, when it would discover one element out of which all others could be made. Physics would stop when it would be able to fulfil its services in discovering one energy of which all the others are but manifestations, and the science of religion become perfect when it would discover Him who is the one life in a universe of death, Him who is the constant basis of an ever-changing world. One who is the only soul of which all souls are but delusive manifestations. Thus is it, through multiplicity and duality, that the ultimate unity is reached. Religion can go no farther. This is the goal of all science.

All science is bound to come to this conclusion in the long run. Manifestation, and not creation, is the word of science today, and the Hindu is only glad that what he has been cherishing in his bosom for ages is going to be taught in more forcible language, and with further light from the latest conclusions of science.

...To the Hindu, then, the whole world of religions is only a travelling, a coming up of different men and women through various conditions and circumstances to the same goal. Every religion is only evolving a God out of the material man, and the same God is the inspirer of all of them. Why, then, are there is so many contradictions? They are only apparent, says the Hindu. The contradictions come from the same truth adapting itself to the varying circumstances of different natures.

It is the same light coming through glasses of different colours. And these little variations are necessary for the purposes of adaptation. But in the heart of everything the same truth reigns. The Lord has declared to the Hindu in His incarnation as Krishna, *I am in every religion as the thread through a string of pearls. Wher-ever thou seest extraordinary holiness and extraordinary power raising and purifying humanity, know thou that I am there.*

...Bold has been my message to the people of the West, bolder is my message to you, my beloved countrymen. The message of ancient India to new Western nations I have tried my best to voice-ill done or well done the future is sure to show. But the mighty voice of the same future is already sending forward soft but distinct murmurs, gaining strength as the days go by, the message of India that is to be to India as she is at present.

Many wonderful institutions and customs, and many wonderful manifestations of strength and power, it has been my good fortune to study in the midst of the various races I have seen, but the most wonderful of all was to find that beneath all these apparent variations of manners and customs, of culture and power, beats the same mighty human heart under the imposition of the same joys and sorrows, of the same weakness and strength.

Good and evil are everywhere and the balance is wondrously even, but above all is the glorious soul of man everywhere which never fails to understand anyone who knows how to speak its own language. Men and women are to be found in every race whose lives are blessings to humanity, verifying the words of the Divine Emperor Ashoka, "In every land dwell Brahmins and Shramanas".

I am grateful to the lands of the West for the many warm hearts that received me with all the love that pure and disinterested souls alone could give. But my life's allegiance is to this my

Motherland, and if I had a thousand lives, every moment of the whole series would be consecrated to your service, my countrymen, my friends.

For to the land I owe whatever I possess, physical, mental and spiritual, and if I have been successful in anything, the glory is yours, not mine. Mine alone are my weaknesses and failures, as they come through my inability of profiting by the mighty lessons with which this land surrounds one, even from his very birth.

And what a land! Whosoever stands on this sacred land, whether alien or a child of the soil, feels himself surrounded-unless his soul is degraded to the level of brute animals-by the living thoughts of the earth's best and purest sons, who have been working to raise the animal to the Divine through centuries whose beginning history fails to trace. The very air is full of the pulsations of spirituality. This land is sacred to philosophy, to ethics and spirituality, to all that tends to give a respite to man in his incessant struggle for the preservation of the animal, to all training that makes man throw off the garment of brutality and stand revealed as the Spirit immortal, the birthless, the deathless, he everblessed-the land where the cup of pleasure was full, and fuller has been the cup of misery, until here, first of all, man found out that it was all vanity; here first of all, in the prime of youth, in the lap of luxury, in the height of glory and plenitude of power, he broke through the fetters of delusion. Here in this ocean of humanity, amidst the sharp interaction of strong currents of pleasure and pain, of strength and weakness of wealth and poverty, of joy and sorrow, of smile and tear, of life and death, in the melting rhythm of eternal peace and calmness, arose the throne of renunciation! Here in this land, the great problems of life and death, of the thirst for life, and the vain mad struggles to preserve it only resulting in the accumulation of woes, were first grappled with and solved—solved as they never were before and never will be hereafter; for here, and here alone was discovered, that even life itself is an evil, the shadow only of something which alone is real. This is the land where alone religion was practical and real and here alone men and women plunged boldly into realise the goal, just as in other lands they madly plunge into realise the pleasures of life, by robbing their weaker brethren. Here, and here, alone the human heart expanded till it included not only the human, but birds, beasts, and plants, from the highest gods to grains of sand, the highest and the lowest, all find a place in the heart of man, grown great, infinite. And here alone, the human soul studied the universe as one unbroken unity whose every pulse was his own pulse.

We all hear so much about the degradation of India. There was a time when I also believed in it. But today standing on the vantage-ground of experience, with eyes cleared of obstructive predispositions and above all, of the highly coloured pictures of other countries toned down to their proper shade and light by actual contact, I confess, in all humility, that I was wrong. Thou blessed land of the Aryas, thou wast never degraded. Sceptres have been broken and thrown away, the ball of power has passed from hand to hand but in India, courts and kings always touched only a few; the vast mass of the people, from the highest to the lowest, has been left to pursue its own inevitable course, the current of national life flowing at time slow and half-conscious, at others, strong and awakened. I stand in awe before the unbroken procession of scores of shining centuries, with here and there a dim link in the chain, only to flare up with added brilliance in the next and there she is walking with her own majestic steps-my motherland-to fulfil her glorious destiny, which no power on earth or in heaven can check—the regeneration of man the brute into man the God.

Aye, a glorious destiny, my brethren, for as far back as the days of the Upanishads we have thrown the challenge to the world- "Not by wealth, not by progeny, but by renunciation alone immortality is reached." Race after race has taken the challenge up, and tried their utmost to solve the world-riddle on the plane of desires. They have all failed in the past, the old ones have become extinct under the weight of wickedness and misery, which lust for power and gold brings in its train, and the new ones are tottering to their fall. The question has yet to be decided whether peace will survive or war; whether patience will survive or non-forbearance, whether goodness will survive or wickedness; whether muscle will survive or brain; whether worldliness will survive or spirituality. We have solved our problem ages ago, and held on to it through good or evil fortune, and mean to hold on to it until the end of time. Our solution is unworldliness-renunciation.

This is the theme of Indian life-work, the burden of her eternal sons, the backbone of her existence, the foundation of her being, the raison d'etre of her very existence–the spiritualisation of the human race. In her life course she has never deviated, whether the Tartar ruled or the Turk, whether the Mogul ruled or the English.

And I challenge anybody to show one single period of her national life when India was lacking in spiritual giants, capable of moving the world. But her work is spiritual, and that cannot be done with blasts of war-trumpets or the march of cohorts. Her influence has always fallen upon the world like that of the gentle dew, unheard and scarcely marked, yet bringing into bloom the fairest flowers of the earth. This influence being in its nature gentle, would have to wait for a fortunate combination of circumstances, to go out of the country into other lands, though it never ceased to work within the limits of its native land. As such, every educated person knows that whenever the empire-building Tartar or Persian or Greek or Arab brought this land in contact with the outside world, a mass of spiritual influence immediately flooded the world from here. The very same circumstances have presented themselves once more before us. The English high-roads over land and sea and the wonderful power manifested by the inhabitants of that little island, have once more brought India in contact with the rest of the world, and the same work has already begun. Mark my words, this is but the small beginning, big things are to follow; what the result of the present work outside India will be I cannot exactly state, but this I know for certain, that millions, I say deliberately, millions in every civilised land are waiting for the message that will save them for the hideous abyss of materialism into which modern money-worship is driving them headlong, and many of the leaders of the new social movements have already discovered, that Vedanta in its highest form can alone spiritualise their social aspirations. I shall have to return to this towards the end. I take up therefore the other great subject, the work within the country.

The problem assumes a twofold aspect, not only spiritualisation but assimilation of the various elements of which the nation is composed. The assimilation of different races into one has been the common task in the life of every nation.

Amongst all races of the world, form the earliest time in history, India has been called the land of wisdom. For ages India itself has never gone out to conquer other nations. Its people have never been fighters. Unlike your Western people, they do not eat meat, as meat makes fighters; the blood of animals makes you restless and you desire to do something.

Compare India and England in the Elizabethan period. What a dark age it was for your people and how enlightened we were even then. The Anglo-Saxon people have always been badly fitted for art. They have good poetry for instance, how wonderful is the blank verse of Shakespeare. Merely the rhyming of words is not good; it is the most uncivilised thing in the world.

In India, music was developed to the full seven notes: even to half and quarter notes, ages ago, India led in music, also in drama and sculpture. Whatever is done now is merely an attempt at imitation. Everything now in India hinges on the question of how little a man requires living upon.

The philosophy of India percolates throughout the whole civilised world, modifying and permeating as it goes. So also in ancient times, her trade reached the shores of Africa before Europe was known and opened communication with the rest of the world, thus disproving the belief that Indians never went outside of their own country.

It is remarkable also that the possession of Indian by a foreign power has always been a turning point in the history of that power, bringing to it wealth, prosperity, dominion and spiritual ideas. While the Western man tries to measure how much it is possible for him to possess and to enjoy, the Eastern seems to take the opposite course, and to measure how little of material possessions he can do with. In the Vedas we trace the endeavour of that ancient people to find God. In their search for Him they came upon different strata beginning with ancestor worship, they passed on to the worship of Agni, the Fire God, of Indra, the God of thunder, and of Varuna, the God of gods. We find the growth of this idea of God, from many gods to one God, in all religions; its real meaning is that he is the chief of the tribal gods, who creates the world, rules it and sees into every heart; the stages of growth lead up from a multiplicity of gods to monotheism. This anthropomorphic conception, however, did not satisfy the Hindus, it was too human for them who were seeking the Divine. Therefore they finally gave up searching for God in the outer world of sense and matter, and turned their attention to the inner world. Is there an inner world? And what is it? It is Atman. It is the Self, it is the only thing an individual can be sure of. If he knows himself, he can know the universe, and not otherwise. The same question was asked in the beginning of time, even in the Rig Veda, in another form: "Who or what existed from the beginning?" That question was gradually solved by the Vedanta philosophy. The Atman existed. That is to say, what we call the Absolute, the Universal Soul, the Self, is the Force by which from the beginning all things have been and are and will be manifested.

While the Vedanta philosophers solved that question, they at the same time discovered the basis of ethics. Though all religions have taught ethical precepts, such as, "do not kill do not injure; love your neighbour as yourself," etc. Yet none of these has given the reason. Why should I not injure my neighbour? To this question there was no satisfactory or conclusive answer forthcoming, until it was evolved by the metaphysical speculations of the Hindus who could not rest satisfied with mere dogmas. So the Hindus say, that this Atman is absolute and all pervading, therefore infinite. There cannot be two infinites for they would limit each other and would become finite. Also each individual soul is a part and parcel of that Universal Soul, which is infinite. Therefore in injuring his neighbour, the individual actually injures himself. This is the basic metaphysical truth underlying all ethical codes. It is often believed that a person in his progress towards perfection passes from error to truth; that when he passes on from one thought to another, he must necessarily reject the first. But no error can lead to truth. The soul passing through its different stages goes from truth to truth, and each stage is true; it goes from lower truth to higher truth. This point may be illustrated in the following way. A man is journeying towards the sun and take a photograph at each step, how different would be the first photograph from the second and still more from the third or the last, when he reaches the real sun! But all these, though differing so widely from each other, are true, only they are made to appear different by the changing conditions of time and space. It is the recognition of this truth, which has enabled the Hindus to perceive the universal truth of all religions, from the lowest to the highest; it has made of them the only people who never had religious persecutions. The shrine of a Mohammedan saint which is at the present day neglected and forgotten by Mohammedans, is worshipped by Hindus! Many instances may be quoted, illustrating the same spirit of tolerance.

The Eastern mind could not rest satisfied till it had found that goal which is the end sought by all humanity, namely, Unity. The Western scientist seeks for unity in the atom or the molecule. When he finds it, there is nothing further for him to discover, and so when we find that unity of soul or self, which is called Atman, we can go no further. It becomes clear that everything in the sense-world is a manifestation of that one substance.

I came here to represent a philosophy of India, which is called the Vedanta philosophy. This philosophy is very, very ancient, it is the outcome of that mass of ancient time. Aryan literature is known by the name of the Vedas. It is as it were, the very flower of all the speculations and experiences and analyses, embodied in that mass of literature-collected and culled through centuries. This Vedanta philosophy has certain peculiarities. In the first place, it is perfectly impersonal, it does not owe its origin to any person or prophet; it does not build, itself around one man as a centre. Yet it has nothing to say against philosophies, which do build themselves around certain persons. In later days in India, other philosophies and systems arose, built around certain persons-suit as Buddhism, or many of our present sects. They each have a certain leader to whom they owe allegiance, just as the Christians and Mohammedans have. But the Vedanta philosophy stands as the background of all these various sects, and there is no fight and no antagonism between the Vedanta and any other system in the world.

One principle it lays down-and that, the Vedanta claims is to be found in every religion in the world-that man is divine, that all this which we see around us is the outcome of that consciousness of the divine power. Everything that is strong, and good, and powerful in human nature is the outcome of that divinity, and though potential in many, there is no difference between man and man essentially, all being alike divine. There is as it were, an infinite ocean behind, and you and I are so many waves, coming out of that infinite ocean, and each one of us is trying our best to manifest that infinite outside. So, potentially, each one of us has that infinite ocean of existence, knowledge, and bliss as our birthright, our real nature, and the difference between us is caused by the greater or lesser power to manifest that divine. Therefore the Vedanta lays down that each man should be treated not as what he manifests, but as what he stands for. Each human being stands for the divine, and therefore every teacher should be helpful, not by condemning man, but by helping him to call forth the divinity that is within him.

It also teaches that all the vast mass of energy that we see displayed in society and in every plane of action is really from inside out and therefore what is called inspiration by other sects, the Vedantist begs the liberty to call the expiration of man. At the same time it does not quarrel with other sects, the Vedanta has no quarrel with those who do not understand this divinity of man. Consciously or unconsciously, every man is trying to unfold that divinity.

Man is like an infinite spring, coiled up in a small box, and that spring is trying to unfold itself, and all the social phenomena that we see are the result of this trying to unfold. All the competitions and struggles and evils that we see around us are neither the causes of these unfoldments nor the effects. As one of our great philosophers says-in the case of the irrigation of a field, the tank is somewhere up on a higher level, and the water is trying to rush into the field, and is barred by a gate. But as soon as the gate is opened, the water rushes in by its own nature and if there is dust and dirt in the way, the water rolls over them. But dust and dirt are neither the result nor the cause of this unfolding of the divine nature of man. They are co-existent circumstances, and therefore can be remedied.

Now, this idea, claims the Vedanta, is to be found in all religions, whether in India or outside of it; only in some of them, the idea, is expressed through mythology, and in others, through symbology. The Vedanta claims that there has not been one religious inspiration, one manifestation of the divine man, however great, but it has been the expression of that infinite oneness in human nature; and all that we call ethics and morality and doing good to others, is also but the manifestation of this oneness. There are moments when every man feels that he is one with the universe, and he rushes forth to express it, whether he knows it or not. This expression of oneness is what we call love and sympathy and it is the basis of all our ethics and morality. This is summed up in the Vedanta philosophy by the celebrated aphorism. Tat Tvam Asi, "Thou art That".

To every man, this is taught: Thou art one with this Universal Being, and as such, every soul, that exists, is your soul, and every body that exists, is your body and in hurting any one, you hurt yourself, in loving any one you love yourself. As soon as a current of hatred as thrown outside, whomsoever else it hurts, it also hurts yourself; and if love comes out from you, it is bound to come back to you. For I am the universe; this universe is my body. I am the infinite, only I am not conscious of it now; but I am struggling to get this consciousness of the infinite, and perfection will be reached when full consciousness of this infinite comes.

Another peculiar idea of the Vedanta is that we must allow this infinite variation in religious thought and not try to bring everybody to the same opinion, because the goal is the same. As the Vedantist says in his poetical language, "As so many rivers, having their sources in different mountains, roll down, crooked or straight, and at last come into the ocean—so, all these various creeds and religions, taking their start from different standpoints and running through crooked or straight courses, at last come unto THEE."

As a manifestation of that we find that this most ancient philosophy, through its influence, directly inspired Buddhism, the first missionary religion of the world, and indirectly, it has also influenced Christianity, through the Alexandrians, the Gnostics, and the European philosophers of the middle ages. And later, influencing German thought, it has produced almost a revolution in the regions of philosophy and psychology. Yet all this mass of influence has been given to the world almost unperceived. As the gentle falling of the dew at night brings support to all vegetable life, so, slowly and imperceptibly, this divine philosophy has been spread through the world for the good of mankind. No march of armies has been used to preach this religion. In Buddhism, one of the most missionary religion of the world, we find inscriptions remaining of the great Emperor Asoka recording how missionaries were sent to Alexandria, to Antioch, to Persia, to China, and to various other countries of the then civilised world. Three hundred years before Christ, instructions were given them not to revile other religions: "The basis of all religions is the same, wherever they are; try to help them all you can, teach them all you can, but do not try to injure them."

Thus in India there never was any religious persecution by the Hindus, but only that wonderful reverence, which they have for all the religions of the world. They sheltered a portion of the Hebrews, when they were driven out of their own country; and the Malabar Jews remain as a result. They received at another time the remnant of the Persians when they were almost annihilated; and they remain to this day, as a part of us and loved by us, as the modern Parsees of Bombay. There were Christians who claimed to have come with St. Thomas, the disciple of Jesus Christ; and they were allowed to settle in India and hold their own opinions; and a colony of them is even now in existence in India and this spirit of toleration has not died out. It will not and cannot die there.

This is one of the great lessons that the Vedanta has to teach. Knowing that, consciously or unconsciously we are struggling to reach the same goal, why should we be impatient? If one man is slower than another, we need not be impatient, we need not curse him or revile him. When our eyes are opened and the heart is purified with the work of the same divine influence, the unfolding of the same divinity in every human heart will become manifest; and then alone we shall be in a position to claim the brotherhood of man.

When a man has reached the highest, when he sees neither man nor woman, neither sect nor creed, neither colour nor birth, not any of these differentiations, but goes beyond and finds that divinity which is the real man behind every human being then alone he has reached the universal brotherhood, and that man alone is a Vedantist.

Such are some of the practical historical results of the Vedanta.

...We have nearly finished the metaphysical portion of the Advaita. One point, and perhaps the most difficult to understand, remains. We have seen so far that according to the Advaita theory, all we see around us, and the whole universe in fact is the evolution of that one Absolute. This is called in Sanskrit "Brahman". The Absolute has become changed into the whole of nature. But here comes a difficulty. How is it possible for the Absolute to change? What made the Absolute to change? By its very definition is the Absolute is unchangeable. Change of the unchangeable would be a contradiction. The same difficulty applies to those who believe in a Personal God. For instance, how did this creation arise? It could not have arisen out of nothing; that would be a contradiction—something coming out of nothing can never be. The effect is the cause in another form. Out of the seed, the big tree grows; the tree is the seed, plus air and water taken in. And if there were any method of testing the amount of the air, and water taken to make the body of the tree, we should find that it is exactly the same as the effect, the tree. Modern science has proved beyond doubt that it is so, that the cause is the effect in another form. The adjustment of the parts of the cause changes and becomes the effect. So, we have to avoid this difficulty of having a universe without a cause, and we are bound to admit that God has become the universe.

But we have avoided one difficulty, and landed in another. In every theory, the idea of God comes through the idea of unchangeability. We have traced historically how the one idea which we have always in mind in the search of God, even in its crudest form, is the idea of freedom; and the idea of freedom and of unchangeability is one and the same. It is the free alone which never changes, and the unchangeable alone which is free; for change is produced by something exterior to a thing, or within itself, which is more powerful than the surroundings. Everything which can be changed is necessarily bound by certain cause or causes, which cannot be unchangeable. Supposing God has become this universe, then God is here and has changed. And suppose the Infinite has become this finite universe, so much of the Infinite has gone, and, therefore, God is Infinite minus the universe. A changeable God would be no God. To avoid this doctrine of pantheism, there is a very bold theory of the Vedanta. It is that this universe as we know and think it does not exist, that the unchangeable has not changed, that the whole of this universe is mere appearance and not reality, that this idea of parts, and little beings, and differentiations are only apparent, not the nature of the thing itself. God has not changed at all, and has not become the universe at all. We see God as the universe, because we have to look through time, space and causation. It is time, space and causation that make this differentiation apparently, but not really. This is a very bold theory indeed. Now this theory ought to be explained a little more clearly. It does not mean idealism in the sense in which it is generally understood. It does not say that this universe does not exist; it exists, but at the same time it is not what we take it for. To illustrate this, the example given by the Advaita philosophy is well known. In the darkness of night, a stump of a tree is looked upon as a ghost by some superstitious person, as a policeman by a robber, as a friend by someone waiting for his companion. In all these cases, the stump of the tree did not change, but there are apparent changes and these changes were in the minds of those who saw it. From the subjective side we can understand it better through psychology. There is something outside of ourselves, the true nature of which is unknown and unknowable to us; let us call it x. And there is something inside, which is also unknown and unknowable to us; let us call it y. The knowable in a combination of x plus y, and everything that we know, therefore, must have two parts, the x outside and the y inside; and the x plus y is the thing we know. So, every form in the universe is partly our creation and partly something outside. Now what the Vedanta holds is that this x and this y are one and the same.

A very similar conclusion has been arrived at by some western philosophers, especially by Herbert Spencer and some other modern philosophers. When it is said that the same power which is manifesting itself in the flower is welling up in my own consciousness, it is the very same idea which the Vedantist wants to preach, that the reality of the external world and the reality of the internal world are one and the same. Even the ideas of the internal and external exist by differentiation and do not exist in the things themselves. For instance, if we develop another sense, the whole world will change for us, showing that it is the subject which will change the object. If I change the external world changes. The theory of the Vedanta, therefore, comes to this, that you and I, and everything in the universe are that Absolute, not parts, but the whole. You are the whole of that Absolute, and so are all others, because the idea of part cannot come into it. These divisions, these limitations, are only apparent, not in the thing itself. I am complete and perfect, and I was never bound, boldly preaches the Vedanta. If you think you are bound, bound you will remain; if you know that you are free, free you are. Thus the end and aim of this philosophy is to let us know that we have been free always, and shall remain free for ever. We never change, we never die, and we are never born. What are all these changes then? What becomes of this phenomenal world? This world is ad-mitted as an apparent world, bound by time, space and causation, and it comes to what is called the Vivarta-vada in Sanskrit, evolution of nature, and manifestation of the Absolute. The Absolute does not change, or reevolve. In the little amoeba is that infinite perfection latent. It is called amoeba from its amoeba covering, and from the amoeba to the perfect man the change is not in what is inside—that remains the same, unchangeable—but the change occurs in the covering.

There is a screen here, and some beautiful scenery outside. There is a small hole in the screen through which we can only catch a glimpse of it. Suppose this hole begins to increase; as it grows larger and larger, more and more of the scenery comes into view, and when the screen has vanished, we come face to face with the whole of the scenery. This scene outside is the soul, and the screen between us and the scenery is maya—time, space, and causation. There is a little hole somewhere, through which I can catch only a glimpse of the soul. When the hole is bigger, I see more and more, and when the screen is vanished, I know that I am the soul. So changes in the universe are not in the Absolute; they are in nature. Nature evolves more and more, until the Absolute manifests itself. In everyone it exists; in some it is manifested more than in others. The whole universe is really one. In speaking of the soul, to say that one is superior to another has no meaning. In speaking of the soul, to say that man is superior to the animal or the plant, has no meaning; the whole universe is one. In plants the obstacle to soul-manifestation is very great; in animals a little less; and in man still less; in cultured, spiritual men still less; and in perfect men, it has vanished altogether. All our struggles, exercises, pains, pleasures, tears, and smiles, all that we do and think tend towards that goal, the tearing up of the screen, making the hole bigger, thinning the layers that remain between the manifestation and the reality behind. Our work, therefore, is not to make the soul free, but to get rid of the bondages. The sun is covered by layers of clouds, but remains unaffected by them. The work of the wind is to drive the clouds away, and the more the clouds disappear, the more the light of the sun appears. There is no change whatsoever in the soul—infinite, absolute, eternal, knowledge, bliss, and Existence, neither can there, he birth or death for the soul. Dying, and being born, reincarnation, and going to heaven, cannot be for the soul. These are different appearances, different mirages, different dreams. If a man who is dreaming of this world now dreams of wicked thoughts and wicked deeds, after a certain time the thought of that very dream will produce the next dream. He will dream that he is in a horrible place, being tortured. The man who is dreaming good thoughts and good deeds, after that period of dream is over, will dream he is in a better place; and so on from dream to dream. But the time will come when the whole of this dream will vanish. To everyone of us there must come a time when the whole universe will be found to have been a mere dream, when we shall find that the soul is infinitely better than its surroundings. In this struggle through what we call our environments, there will come a time when we shall find that these environments were almost zero in comparison with the power of the soul. It is only a question of time, and time is nothing in the Infinite. It is a drop in the ocean. We can afford to wait and be calm.

Consciously or unconsciously, therefore, the whole universe is going towards that goal. The moon is struggling to get out of the sphere of attraction of other bodies, and will come out of it, in the long run. But those who consciously strive to get free hasten the time. One benefit from this theory we practically see is that the idea of a real universal love is only possible from this point of view. All are our fellow passengers, our fellow travellers—all life, plants, animals; not only my brother man, but my brother brute, my brother plant; not only my brother the good, but my brother the evil, my brother the spiritual and my brother the wicked. They are all going to the same goal. All are in the same stream, each is hurrying towards that infinite freedom. We cannot stay the course, none can stay it, none can go back, however he may try; he will be driven forward, and in the end he will attain to freedom. Creation means the struggle to get back to freedom, the centre of our being, whence we have been thrown off, as it were. The very fact that we are here, shows that we are going towards the centre, and the manifestation of this attraction towards the centre is what we call love.

The question is asked: From where does this universe come, in what does it remain, to where does it go back? And the answer is: From love it comes, in love it remains, back it goes unto love. Thus we are in a position to understand that, whether one likes it or not, there is no going back for anyone. Everyone has to get to the centre, however he may struggle to go back. Yet if we struggle consciously, knowingly, it will smooth the passage, it will lessen the jar, and quicken the time. Another conclusion we naturally arrive at from this is that all knowledge and all power are within but not without. When we call nature is a reflecting glass—that is all the use of nature—and all knowledge is this reflection of the within on this glass of nature. What we call powers, secrets of nature, and force, are all within. In the external world are only a series of changes. There is no knowledge in nature; all knowledge comes from the human soul. Man manifests knowledge, discovers it within himself, which is pre-existing through eternity. Everyone is the embodiment of knowledge, everyone is the embodiment of eternal bliss, and eternal existence. The ethical effect is just the same, as we have seen elsewhere, with regard to equality.

But the idea of privilege is the bane of human life. Two forces, as it were, are constantly at work one making caste and the other breaking caste; in other words, the one making for privilege and the other breaking down privilege. And whenever privilege is broken down, more and more light and progress come to a race. This struggle we see all around us. Of course this is the first brutal idea of privilege, that of the strong over the weak. There is the privilege of wealth. If a man has more money than another, he wants a little privilege over those who have less. There is the still subtler and more powerful privilege of intellect because one man knows more than others, he claims more privilege. And the last of all, and the worst, because the most tyrannical is the privilege of spirituality. If some persons think they know more of spirituality, of God, they claim a superior privilege over everyone else. They say, "Come down and worship us, ye common herds; we are the messengers of God, and you have to worship us." None can be Vedantists, and at the same time admit of privilege to anyone, either mental, physical, or spiritual; absolutely no privilege for anyone. The same power is in every man, the one manifesting more, the other less; the same potentiality is in everyone. Where is the claim to privilege? All knowledge is in every soul, even in the most ignorant; he has not manifested it, but perhaps, he has not had the opportunity, the environments were not perhaps suitable to him. When he gets the opportunity, he will manifest it. The idea that one man is born superior to another has no meaning in the Vedanta; that between two nations one is superior and the other inferior has no meaning whatsoever. Put them in the same circumstances, and see whether the same intelligence comes out or not. Before that you have no right to say that one nation is superior to another. And as to spirituality, no privilege should be claimed there. It is a privilege to serve mankind, for this is the worship of God. God is here, in all these human souls. He is the soul of man. What privilege can men ask? There are no special messengers of God, never were, and never can be. All beings, great or small, are equally manifestations of God; the difference is only in the manifestation. The same eternal message, which has been eternally given, comes to them little by little. The eternal message has been written in the heart of every being; it is there already, and all are struggling to express it. Some in suitable circumstances express it a little better than others, but as bearers of the message they are all one. What claim to superiority is there? The most ignorant man, the most ignorant child is as great a messenger of God as any that ever existed, and as great as any that are yet to come. For the infinite message is there imprinted once for all in the heart of every being. Wherever here is a being, that being contains the infinite message of the most high. It is there. The work of the Advaita, therefore, is to break down all these privileges. It is the hardest work of all, and curious to say, it has been less active than anywhere else in the land of its birth. If there is any land of privilege, it is the land which gave birth to this philosophy—privilege for the spiritual man as well as for the man of birth. There they have not so much privilege for money (that is one of the benefits, I think), but privilege for birth and spirituality is everywhere.

Once a gigantic attempt was made to preach Vedantic ethics, which succeeded to a certain extent for several hundred years, and we know historically that those years were the best times of that nation. I mean the Buddhistic attempt to break down privilege. Some of the most beautiful epithets addressed to Buddha that I remember are, "Thou the breaker of castes, destroyer of privileges, preacher of equality to all beings". So, he preached this one idea of equality. Its power has been misunderstood to a certain extent in the brotherhood of Shramanas, where we find that hundreds of attempts have been made to make them into a church, with superiors and inferiors. You cannot make much of a church when you tell people they are all gods. One of the good effects of Vedanta has been freedom of religious thought, which India enjoyed throughout all times of its history. It is something to glory in, that it is the land where there was never a religious persecution, where people are allowed perfect freedom in religion.

This practical side of Vedanta morality is necessary as much today as it ever was, more necessary, perhaps, than it ever was, for all this privilege claiming has become tremendously intensified with the extension of knowledge. The idea of the God and the devil, or Ahura Mazda and Ahriman, has a good deal of poetry in it. The difference between the God and the devil is in nothing except in unselfishness and selfishness. The devil knows as much as God, is as powerful as God; only he has no holiness—that makes him a devil. Applying the same idea to the modern world: excess of knowledge and power, without holiness, makes human beings devils. Tremendous power is being acquired by the manufacturers of machines and other appliances, and privilege is claimed today as it never has been claimed in the history of the world. That is why, the Vedanta wants to preach against it, to break down this tyrannising over the souls of men.

Those of you who have studied the Gita will remember the memorable passages: "He who looks upon the learned Brahmin upon the cow, the elephant, the dog, or the outcaste with the same eye, he indeed is the sage, and the wise man"; "Even in this life he has conquered the relative existence whose mind is firmly fixed on this sameness, for the Lord is one and the same to all, and the Lord is pure; therefore, those who have this sameness for all, and are pure, are said to be living in the God." This is the gist of the Vedantic morality—this sameness for all. We have seen that it is the subjective world that rules the objective one. Change the subject, and the object is bound to change; purify yourself, and the world is bound to be purified. This one thing requires to be taught now more than ever before. We are becoming more and more enquisitive about our neighbours, and less and less about ourselves. The world will change if we change; if we are pure, the world will become pure. The question is why I should see evil in others I cannot see evil unless I an evil. I cannot be miserable unless I am weak. The things that used to make me miserable when I was a child, do not do so now. The subject changed, so the object was bound to change; so says the Vedanta. All these things which we call causes of misery and evil, we shall laugh at when we arrive at that wonderful state of equality, that sameness. This is what is called in Vedanta attaining to freedom. The sign of approaching that freedom is more and more of this sameness and equality. In misery and happiness the same, in success and defeat the same—such a mind is nearing that state of freedom.

The mind cannot be easily conquered. Minds that rise into waves at the approach of every little thing at the slightest provocation or danger, in what a state they must be What to talk of greatness or spirituality, when these changes come over the mind? This unstable condition of the mind must be changed. We must ask ourselves how far we can be acted upon by the external world, and how far we can stand on our own feet, in spite of all the forces outside us. When we have succeeded in preventing all the forces in the world from throwing us off our balance, then alone we have attained to freedom, and not before. That is salvation. It is here and nowhere else; it is this moment. Out of this idea, out of this fountain-head, all beautiful streams of thought have flowed upon the world, generally misunderstood in their expression, apparently contradicting each other. We find hosts of brave and wonderfully spiritual souls, in every nation, taking to caves or forests for meditation, severing their connection with the external world. This is the one idea. And, on the other hand, we find bright, illustrious beings coming into society, trying to raise their fellow men, the poor, the miserable. Apparently these two methods are contradictory. The man who lives in a cave, apart from his fellow-beings, smiles contemptuously upon those who are working for the regeneration of their fellow men. "How foolish!" he says; "what work is there? The world of Maya will always remain the world of Maya; it cannot be changed." If I ask one of our priests in India, "Do you believe in Vedanta?"—he says, "That is my religion; I certainly do; that is my life," "Very well, do" you admit the equality of all life, the sameness of everything?" "Certainly, I do." The next moment, when a low-caste man approaches this priest, he jumps to one side of the street to avoid that man. "Why do you jump?" "Because his very touch would have polluted me." "But you were just saying we are all the same, and you admit there is no difference in souls." He says, "Oh, that is in theory only for householders; when I go into a forest, then I will look upon everyone as the same" You ask one of your great men in England, of great birth and wealth, if he believes as a Christian in the brotherhood of mankind, since all came from God. He answers in the affirmative, but in five minutes he shouts something uncomplimentary about the common herd. Thus, it has been a theory only for several thousand years and never came into practice. All understand it, declare it as the truth, but when you ask them to practise it, they say, it will take millions of years. There was a certain king who had a huge number of courtiers, and each one of these courtiers declared he was ready to sacrifice his life for his master, and that he was the most sincere being ever born. In course of time, a *Sannyasin* came to the king. The king said to him that there never was a king who had so many sincere courtiers as he had. The *Sannyasin* smiled and said he did not believe that. The king said the *Sannyasin* could test it if he liked. So the *Sannyasin* declared that he would make a great sacrifice by which the king's reign would be extended very long, with the condition that there should be made a small tank into which each one of his courtiers should pour a pitcher of milk, in the dark of night. The king smiled and said, "Is this the test?" And he asked his courtiers to come to him, and told them what was to be done. They all expressed their joyful assent to the proposal and returned. In the dead of night, they came and emptied their pitchers into the tank. But in the morning, it was found full of water only. The courtiers were assembled and questioned about the matter. Each one of them had thought there would be so many pitchers of milk that his water would not be detected. Unfortunately most of us have the same idea and we do our share of work as did the courtiers in the story.

There is so much idea of equality, says the priest, that my little privilege will not be detected. So say our rich men, so say the tyrants of every country. There is more hope for the tyrannised over, than for the tyrants. It will take a very long time for tyrants to arrive at freedom, but less time for the others. The cruelty of the fox is much more terrible than the cruelty of the lion. The lion strikes a blow and is quiet for some time afterwards, but the fox trying persistently to follow his prey never misses an opportunity. Priestcraft is in its nature cruel and heartless. That is why religion goes down where priestcraft arises. Says the Vedanta, we must give up the idea of privilege, then will religion come. Before that there is no religion at all.

Do you believe what Christ says, "Sell all that thou hast, and give to the poor?" Practical equality there; no trying to torture the texts, but taking the truth as it is. Do not try to torture texts. I have heard it said that that was preached only to the handful of Jews who listened to Jesus. The same argument will apply to other things also. Do not torture texts; dare to face truth as it is. Even if we cannot reach to it, let us confess our weakness, but let us not destroy the ideal. Let us hope that we shall attain to it sometime, and strive for it. There it is— "Sell all that thou hast, and give to the poor, and follow me." Thus, trampling on every privilege and everything in us that works for privilege, let us work for that knowledge which will bring the feeling of sameness towards all mankind. You think that because you talk a little more polished language you are superior to the man in the street. Remember that when you are thinking this, you are not going towards freedom, but are forging a fresh chain for your feet. And, above all, if the pride of spirituality enters into you, woe unto you. It is the most awful bondage that ever existed. Neither can wealth nor any other bondage of the human heart bind the soul so much as this. "I am purer than others", is the most awful idea that can enter into the human heart. In what sense are you pure? The God in you is the God in all. If you have not known this, you have known nothing. How can there be difference? It is all one, Every being is the temple of the Most High; if you can see that, good, if not, spirituality has yet to come to you.

...We have seen how the greater portion of our life must of necessity be filled with evils, however we may resist, and that this mass of evil is practically almost infinite for us. We have been struggling to remedy this since the beginning of time, yet everything remains very much the same. The more we discover remedies, the more we find ourselves beset by subtler evils. We have also seen that all religions propose a God, as the one way of escaping these difficulties. All religions tell us that if you take the world as it is, as most practical people would advise us to do in this age, then nothing would be left to us but evil. They further assert that there is something beyond this world. This life in the five senses, life in the material world, is not all; it is only a small portion, and merely superficial. Behind and beyond is the Infinite in which there is no more evil. Some people call It God, some *Allah*, some *Jehovah*, *Jove*, and so on. The Vedantin calls it Brahman.

The first impression we get of the advice given by religions is that we had better terminate our existence. To the question how to cure the evils of life, the answer apparently is, give up life. It reminds one of the old story A mosquito settled on the head of a man, and a friend, wishing to kill the mosquito, gave it such a blow that he killed both man and mosquito. The remedy of evil seems to suggest a similar course of action. Life is full of ills, the world is full of evils; that is a fact no one who is old enough to know the world can deny.

But what is remedy proposed by all the religions? That this world is nothing. Beyond this world is something which is very real. Here comes the difficulty. The remedy seems to destroy everything. How can that be a remedy? Is there no way out then? The Vedanta lays that what all the religions advance is perfectly true, but should be properly understood. Often it is misunderstood, because the religions are not very dear in their meaning. What we really want is head and heart combined. The heart is great indeed; it is through the heart that come the great inspirations of life, I would a hundred times rather have a little heart and no brain, than be all brains and no heart. Life is possible, progress is possible for him who has heart, but he who has no heart and only brains dies of dryness.

At the same time, we know that he who is carried along by his heart alone has to undergo many ills, for now and then, he is liable to tumble into pitfalls. The combination of heart and head is what we want. I do not mean that a man should compromise his heart for his brain or vice versa, but let everyone have an infinite amount of heart and feeling, and at the same time an infinite amount of reason. Is there any limit to what we want in this world? Is the world not infinite? There is room for an infinite amount of feeling, and so also for an infinite amount of culture and reason. Let them come together without limits let them run together, as it were, parallel to each other.

Most of the religions understand the fact, but the error into which they all seem to fall is the same; they are carried away by the heart, the feelings. There is evil in the world, give up the world; that is the great teaching, and the only teaching, undoubtedly. Give up the world. There cannot be two opinions of understanding the truth. Everyone of us has to give up error. There cannot be two opinions as in everyone of us in order to have good must give up evil; there cannot be two opinions as in everyone of us to have life must give up what is death.

And yet, what remains to us, if this theory involves giving up the life of the senses, of the life as we know it? And what else do we mean by life? If we give this up, what remains?

We shall understand this better, when, later on, we come to the more philosophical portions of the Vedanta. But for the present, I beg to state that, in Vedanta alone, we find a rational solution to the problem. Here I can only lay before you what the Vedanta seeks to teach, and that is the deification of the world. The Vedanta does not, in reality, denounce the world. The ideal of renunciation, nowhere, attains such a height as in the teachings of the Vedanta. But, at the same time, dry suicidal advice is not intended; it really means deification of the world; "giving up the world", as we think of it, as we know it, as it appears to us and to know what it really is. Deify it; it is God alone. We read at the commencement of one of the oldest of the Upanishads, "Whatever exists in this universe is to be covered with the Lord".

We have to cover everything with the Lord Himself, not by a false sort of optimism, not by blinding our eyes to the evil, but by really seeing God in everything. Thus we have to give up the world, and when the world is given up, what remains? God. What is meant? You can have your wife; it does not mean that you are to abandon her, but that you are to see God in the wife. Give up your children; what does that mean? To turn them out of doors, as some human brutes do in every country? Certainly not. That is diabolism; it is not religion. But see God in your children. So, in everything. In life and in death, in happiness and in misery, the Lord is equally present. The whole world is full of the Lord. Open your eyes and see Him. This is what Vedanta teaches. Give up the world which you have conjectured, because your conjecture was based upon a very partial experience, upon very poor reasoning, and upon your own weakness.

Give it up; the world we have been thinking of so long, the world to which we have been clinging so long, is a false world of our own creation. Give that up; open your eyes and see that as such it never existed; it was a dream, Maya. What existed was the Lord Himself. It is He who is in the child, in the wife, and in the husband; it is He who is in the good and in the bad; He is in the sin and in the sinner; He is in life and in death.

A tremendous assertion indeed! Yet that is the theme which the Vedanta wants to demonstrate, to teach, and to preach. This is just the opening theme.

Thus we avoid the dangers of life and its evils. Do not desire anything. What makes us miserable? The cause of all miseries from which we suffer is desire. You desire something, and the desire is not fulfilled; the result is distress. If there is no desire, there is no suffering. But here, too, there is the danger of my being misunderstood. So it is necessary to explain what I mean by giving up desire and becoming free from all misery. The walls have no desire and they never suffer. True, but they never evolve. This chair has no desires, it never suffers; but it is always a chair. There is a glory in happiness, there is a glory in suffering. If I may dare to say so, there is a utility in evil too. The great lesson in misery we all know? There are hundreds of things we have done in our lives which we wish we had never done, but which, at the same time, have been great teachers. As for me, I am glad I have done something good and many things bad; glad I have done something right, and glad I have committed many errors, because every one of them has been a great lesson. I, as I am now, am the resultant of all I have done, all I have thought. Every action and thought have had their effect, and these effects are the sum total of my progress.

We all understand that desires are wrong, but what is meant by giving up desires? How could life go on? It would be the same suicidal advice, killing the desire and the man too. The solution is this. Not that you should not have property, not that you should not have things which are necessary and things which are even luxuries. Have all that you want, and more, only know the truth and realise it. Wealth does not belong to anybody. Have no idea of proprietorship, possessorship. You are nobody, nor am I, nor anyone else. All belongs to the Lord, because the opening verse told us to put the Lord in everything. God is in the wealth that you enjoy. He is in the desire that rises in your mind. He is in the things you buy to satisfy your desire; He is in your beautiful attire, in your beautiful ornaments. This is the line of thought. All will be metamorphosed as soon as you begin to see things in that light. If you put God in your every movement, in your conversation, in your form, in everything, the whole scene changes, and the world, instead of appearing as one of woe and misery, will become a heaven.

"The kingdom of heaven is within you," says Jesus; so says the Vedanta, and every great teacher. "He that hath eyes to see, let him see, and he that hath ears to hear, let him hear." The Vedanta proves that the truth for which we have been searching all this time is present, and was all the time with us. In our ignorance, we thought we had lost it, and went about the world crying and weeping, struggling to find the truth, while all along it was dwelling in our own hearts. There alone can we find it.

If we understand the giving up of the world in its old, crude sense, then it would come to this: that we must not work, that we must be idle, sitting like lumps of earth, neither thinking nor doing anything, but must become fatalists, driven about by every circumstance, ordered about by the laws of nature, drifting from place to place. That would be the result. But that is not what is meant. We must work. Ordinary mankind, driven everywhere by false desire, what do they know of work? The man propelled by his own feelings and his own senses, what does he know about work? He works, who is not propelled by his own desires, by any selfishness whatsoever. He works, who has no ulterior motive in view. He works, who has nothing to gain from work.

Who enjoys the picture, the seller or the seer? The seller is busy with his accounts, computing what his gain, will be, how much profit he will realise on the picture. His brain is full of that. He is looking at the hammer, and watching the bids. He is intent on hearing how fast the bids are rising. That man is enjoying the picture who has gone there without any intention of buying or selling. He looks at the picture and enjoys it. So this whole universe is a picture, and when these desires have vanished, men will enjoy the world, and then this buying and selling and these foolish ideas of possession will be ended. The moneylender gone, the buyer gone, the seller gone, this world remains the picture, a beautiful painting. I never read of any more beautiful conception of God than the following: "He is the Great Poet, the Ancient Poet; the whole universe is His poem, coming in verses and rhymes and rhythms, written in infinite bliss."

When we have given up desires, then alone shall we be able to read and enjoy this universe of God. Then everything will become deified. Nooks and corners, byways and shady places, which we thought dark and unholy, will be all deified. They will all reveal their true nature, and we shall smile at ourselves and think that all this weeping and crying has been but child's play, and we were only standing by, watching.

So, do your work, says the Vedanta. It first advises us how to work by giving up giving up the apparent, illusive world. What is meant by that? Seeing God everywhere. Thus do you work. Desire to live a hundred years, have all earthly desires, if you wish, only deify them, convert them into heaven. Have the desire to live a long life of helpfulness, of blissfulness and activity on this earth. Thus working, you will find the way out. There is no other way. If a man plunges headlong into foolish luxuries of the world without knowing the truth, he has missed his footing, he cannot reach the goal. And if a man curses the world, goes into a forest, mortifies his flesh, and kills himself little by little by starvation, makes his heart a barren waste, kills out all feelings, and becomes harsh, stern, and dried up, that man also has missed the way. These are the two extremes, the two mistakes at, either end. Both have lost the way, both have missed: the goal.

So work, says the Vedanta, putting God in everything, and knowing Him to be in everything. Work in-cessantly, holding life as something deified, as God Himself, and knowing that this is all we have to do, this is all we should ask for. God is in everything, where else shall we go to find Him? He is already in every work, in every thought, in every feeling. Thus knowing, we must word this is the only way; there is no other. Thus the effects of work will not bind us. We have seen how false desires are the cause of all the misery and evil we suffer, but when they are thus deified, purified, through God, they bring no evil, they bring no misery. Those who have not learnt this secret will have to live in a demoniacal world until they discover it. Many do not know what an infinite mine of bliss is in them, around them, everywhere; they have not yet discovered it. What is a demoniacal world? The Vedanta says, ignorance.

We are dying of thirst sitting on the banks of the mightiest river. We are dying of hunger sitting near heaps of food. Here is the blissful universe, yet we do not find it. We are in it all the time, and we are always mistaking it. Religion proposes to find this out for us.

The longing for this blissful universe is in all hearts. It has been the search of all nations, it is the one goal of religion, and this ideal is expressed in various languages in different religions. It is only the difference of language that makes all these apparent divergences. One expresses a thought in one way, another a little differently, yet perhaps each is meaning exactly what the other is expressing in a different language.

More questions arise in connection with this. It is very easy to talk. From my childhood I have heard of seeing God everywhere and in everything, and then I can really enjoy the world, but as soon as I mix with the world, and get a few blows from it, the idea vanishes, I am walking in the street thinking that God is in every man, and a strong man comes along and gives me a push and I fall flat on the footpath. Then I rise up quickly with clenched fist, the blood has rushed to my head, and the reflection goes. Immediately I have become mad. Everything is forgotten; instead of encountering God I see the devil. Ever since we were born we have been told to see God in all. Every religion teaches that see God in everything and everywhere. Do you not remember in the New Testament how Christ says so? We have all been taught that; but it is when we come to the practical side, that the difficulty begins. You all remember how in Aesop's Fables a fine stag is looking at his form reflected in a lake and is saying to his young one, "How powerful I am, look at my splendid head, look at my limbs, how strong and muscular they are; and how swiftly I can run." In the meantime he hears the barking of dogs in the distance, and immediately takes to his heels, and after he has run several miles, lie comes back panting. The young one says, "You just told me how strong you were, how was it that when the dog barked, you ran away?" "Yes, my son; but when the dogs bark all my confidence vanishes." Such is the case with us. We think highly of humanity. We feel ourselves strong and valiant, we make grand resolves; but when the "dogs" of trial and temptation bark, we are like the stag in the fable. Then, if such is the case, what is the use of teaching all these things? There is the greatest use. The use is this, that perseverance will finally conquer. Nothing can be done in a day.

"This Self is first to be heard, then to be thought upon, and then meditated upon." Everyone can see the sky, even the very worm crawling upon the earth sees the blue sky, but how very far away it is! So it is with our ideal, It is far away, no doubt, but at the same time, we know that we must have it. We must even have the highest ideal. Unfortunately in this life, the vast majority of persons are groping through this dark life without any ideal at all. If a man with an ideal makes a thousand mistakes, I am sure that the man without an ideal makes fifty thousand. Therefore, it is better to have an ideal. And this ideal we must hear about as much as we can, till it enters into our hearts, into our brains, into our very veins, until it tingles in every drop of our blood and permeates every pore in our body. We must meditate upon it. "Out of the fullness of the heart the mouth speaketh," and out of the fullness of the heart the hand works too.

It is thought which is the propelling force in us. Fill the mind with the highest thoughts, hear them day after day, think them month after month Never mind failures; they are quite natural, they arc the beauty of life, those failures. What would life be without them? It would not be worth having if it were not for struggles. Where would be the poetry of life? Never mind the struggles, the mistakes. I never heard a cow tell a lie, but it is only a cow never a man. So never mind these failures. these little backslidings; hold the ideal a. thousand times, and if you fail a thousand times, make the attempt once more. The ideal of man is to see God in everything. But if you cannot see Him in everything, see Him in one thing, in that thing which you like best, and then see Him in another. So on you can go. There is infinite life before the soul. Take your time and you will achieve your end.

"He, the One, who vibrates more quickly than mind, who attains to more speed than mind can ever do, whom even the gods reach not, nor thought grasps, He moving, everything moves. In Him all exists. He is moving. He is also immovable. He is near and He is far. He is inside everything. He is outside everything, interpenetrating everything. Whoever sees in every being that same Atman, and whoever sees everything in that Atman, he never goes far from that Atman. When all life and the whole universe are seen in this Atman, then alone man has attained the secret. There is no more delusion for him. Where is any more misery for him who sees this Oneness in the universe?"

This is another great theme of the Vedanta, this Oneness of life, this Oneness of everything. We shall see how it demonstrates that all our misery comes through ignorance, and this ignorance is the idea of manifoldncss, this separation between man and man, between nation and nation, between earth and moon, between moon and sun. Out of this idea of separation between atom and atom comes all misery. But the Vedanta says this separation does not exist, it is not real. It is merely apparent, on the surface. In the heart of things there is unity still. If you go below the surface, you find that unity between man and man, between races and races, high and low, rich and poor, gods and men, and men and animals. If you go deep enough, all will be seen as only variations of the one, and he who has attained to this conception of Oneness has no more delusion. What can delude him? He knows the reality of everything, the secret of everything. Where is there any more misery for him? What does he desire? He has traced the reality of everything to the Lord, the Centre, the Unity of everything, and that is eternal existence, eternal knowledge, eternal bliss. Neither death nor disease, nor sorrow, nor misery, nor discontent is there. All is perfect union and perfect bliss. For whom should he mourn then? In the reality, there is no death, there is no misery; in the reality, there is no one to mourn for, no one to be sorry for. He has penetrated everything, the pure one, the formless, the bodiless, the stainless. He the knower, He the great poet, the self-existent, He who is giving to everyone what he deserves. They grope in darkness who worship this ignorant world, the world that is produced out of ignorance, thinking of it as existence, and those who live their whole lives in this world, and never find anything better or higher, are groping in still greater darkness. But he who knows the secret of nature, seeing That which is beyond nature through the help of nature, he crosses death, and through the help of that which is beyond nature, he enjoys Eternal Bliss. "Thou sun, who has covered the Truth with thy golden disc, do thou remove the veil, so that I may sec the Truth that is within thee. I have known the Truth that is within thee, I have known what is the real meaning of thy rays and thy glory and have seen that which shines in thee; the Truth in thee I see, and that which is within thee is within me, and I am that."

..."The Self-existent one projected the senses outwards and, therefore, a man looks outward, not within himself, A certain wise one, desiring immortality, with inverted senses, perceived the Self within." As I have already said, the first inquiry that we find in the Vedas was concerning outward things, and then a new idea came that the reality of things is not to be found in the external world; not by looking outwards, but by turning the eyes, as it is literally expressed, inwards. And the word used for the Soul is very significant: it is He who has gone inward, the innermost reality of our being, the heart centre, the core, from which, as it were, everything comes out; the central sun of which the mind, the body, the senseorgans, and everything else we have are but rays going outwards. "Men of childish intellect, ignorant persons, run after desires which are external, and enter the trap of far-reaching-death, but the wise, understanding immortality, never seek for the eternal in this life of finite things." The same idea is here made clear that in this external world, which is full of finite things, it is impossible to see and find the infinite. The infinite must be sought in that alone which is infinite, and the only thing infinite about us is that which is within us, our own soul. Neither the body, nor the mind, not even our thoughts, nor the world we see around us, are infinite. The Seer, he to whom they all belong, the Soul of man, He who is awake in the internal man, alone is infinite, and to seek for the Infinite Cause of this whole universe we must go there. In the Infinite Soul alone we can find it. "What is here is there too, and what is there is here also. He who sees the manifold goes from death to death." We have seen how at first there was the desire to go to heaven. When these ancient Aryans became dissatisfied with the world around them, they naturally thought that after death they would go to some place where there would be all happiness without any misery; these places they multiplied and called Svargas—the word may be translated as heavens—where there would be joy for ever, the body would become perfect, and also the mind, and there they would live with their forefathers. But as soon as philosophy came, men found that this was impossible and absurd. The very idea of an infinite in place would be a contradiction in terms, as a place must begin and continue in time. Therefore they had to give up that idea. They found out that the gods who lived in these heavens had once been human beings on earth, who through their good works had become gods, and the godhoods, as they call them, were different states, different positions; none of the gods spoken of in the Vedas are permanent individuals.

For instance, Indra and Varuna are not the names of certain persons, but the names of positions as governors and so on. The Indra who had lived before is not the same person as the Indra of the present day; he has passed away, and another man from earth has filled his place. So with all the other gods. These are certain positions, which are filled successively by human souls who have raised themselves to the condition of gods, and yet even they die. In the old Rig-Veda we find the word "immortality" used with regard to these gods, but later on it is dropped entirely, for they found that immortality which is beyond time and space cannot be spoken of with regard to any physical form, however subtle it may be. However fine it may be, it must have a beginning in time and space, for the necessary factors that enter into the make-up of form are in space. Try to think of a form without space: it is impossible. Space is one of the materials, as it were, which make up the form, and this is continually changing space and time are in

Maya, and this idea is expressed in the line— "What is here, that is there too." If there are these gods, they must be bound by the same laws that apply here, and all laws involve destruction and renewal again and again. These laws are moulding matter into different forms, and crushing them out again. Everything born must die; and so, if there are heavens, the same laws must hold good there.

In this world we find that all happiness is followed by misery as its shadow. Life has its shadow, death. They must go together, because they are not contradictory, not two separate existences, but different manifestations of the same unit, life and death, sorrow and happiness, good and evil. The dualistic conception that good and evil are two separate entities, and that they are both going on eternally, is absurd on the face of it. They are the diverse manifestations of one and the same fact, one time appearing as bad, and at another time as good. The difference does not exist in kind, but only in degree. They differ from each other in degree of intensity. We find as a fact that the same nerve systems carry good and bad sensations alike, and when the nerves are injured, neither sensation comes to us. If a certain nerve is paralysed, we do not get the pleasurable feelings that used to come along that wire; and at the same time we do not get the painful feelings either. They are never two, but the same. Again, the same thing produces pleasure and pain at different times of life. The same phenomenon will produce pleasure in one, and pain in another. The eating of meat produces pleasure to a man, but pain to the animal which is eaten. There has never been anything which gives pleasure to all alike. Some are pleased, others displeased. So on it will go. Therefore, this duality of existence is denied. And what follows? I told you in my last lecture that we can never have ultimately everything good on this earth and nothing bad. It may have disappointed and frightened some of you, but I cannot help it, and I am open to conviction when I am shown to the contrary; but until that can be proved to me, and I can find that it is true, cannot say so.

The general argument against my statement, and apparently a very convincing one, is this that in the course of evolution, all that is evil in what we see around us is gradually being eliminated, and the result is that if this elimination continues for millions of years, a time will come when all the evil will have been extirpated, and the good alone will remain. This is apparently a very sound argument. Would to God it were true! But there is a fallacy in it, and it is this that it takes for granted that both good and evil are things that are eternally fixed. It takes for granted that there is a definite mass of evil, which may be represented by a hundred, and likewise of good, and that this mass of evil is being diminished every day, leaving only the good. But is it so? The history of the world shows that evil is a continuously increasing quantity, as well as good. Take the lowest man; he lives in the forest. His sense of enjoyment is very small, and so also is his power to suffer. His misery is entirely on the senseplane. If he does not get plenty of food, he is miserable; but give him plenty of food and freedom to rove and to hunt, and he is perfectly happy. His happiness consists only in the senses, and so does his misery also. But if that man increases in knowledge, his happiness will increase, the intellect will open to him, and his sense-enjoyment will evolve into intellectual enjoyment. He will feel pleasure in reading a beautiful poem, and a mathematical problem will be of absorbing interest to him. But with these, the finer nerves will become more and more susceptible to miseries of mental pain, of which the savage does not think. Take a Very simple illustration. In Tibet there is no marriage, and there is no jealousy, yet we know that marriage is a much higher state. The Tibetans have not known the wonderful enjoyment, the blessing of chastity, the happiness of having a chaste, virtuous wife, or a chaste, virtuous husband. These people cannot feel that, And similarly they do not feel the intense jealousy of the chaste wife or husband, or the misery caused by unfaithfulness on either side, with all the heartburnings and sorrows which believers in chastity experience. On one side, the latter gain happiness, but on the other, they suffer misery too.

Take your country which is the richest in the world, and which is more luxurious than any other, and see how intense is the misery, how many more lunatics you have, compared with other races, only because the desires are o keen, A man must keep up a high standard of living, and the amount of money he spends in one year would be a fortune to a man in India. You cannot preach to him of simple living because society demands so much of him. The wheel of society is rolling on; it stops not for the widow's tears or the orphans' wails. This is the state of things everywhere. Your sense of enjoyment is developed, your society is very much more beautiful than some others. You have so many more things to enjoy. But those who have fewer have much less misery. You can argue thus throughout, the higher the ideal you have in the brain, the greater is your enjoyment, and the more profound your miseri. One is like the shadow of the other. That the evils are being eliminated may be true, but if so, the good also must be dying out. But are not evils multiplying fast, and good diminishing, if I may so put it? If good increases in arithmetical progression, evil increase in geometrical progression. And this is Maya. This is neither optimism nor pessimism. Vedanta does not take the position that this world is only a miserable one. That would be untrue. At the same time, it is a mistake to say that this world is full of happiness and blessings.

So it is useless to tell children that this world is all good, all flowers, all milk and honey. That is what we have all dreamt. At the same time it is erroneous to think, because one man has suffered more than another, that all is evil, It is this duality, this play of good and evil that makes our world of experiences. At the same time the Vedanta says, "Do not think that good and evil are two, are two separate essences, for they are one and the; same thing, appearing in different degrees and in different guises and producing differences of feeling in the same mind." So, the first thought of the Vedanta is the finding of unity in the external; the one existence manifesting itself, however different it may appear in manifestation. Think, of the old crude theory of the Persians—two gods creating this world, the good god doing everything that is good, and the bad one, everything bad. On the very face of it, you see the absurdity, for if it be carried out, every law of nature must have two parts, one of which is manipulated by one god, and then he goes away and the other god manipulates the other part. There the difficulty comes that both are working in the same world, and these two gods keep themselves in harmony by injuring one portion and doing good to another. This is a crude case, of course, the crudest way of expressing the duality of existence. But, take the more advanced, the more abstract theory that this world is partly good and partly bad. This also is absurd, arguing from the same standpoint. It is the law of unity that gives us our food, and it is the same law that kills many through accidents or misadventure.

We find, then, that this world is neither optimistic nor pessimistic; it is a mixture of both, and as we go on we shall find that the whole blame is taken away from nature and put upon our own shoulders. At the same time the Vedanta shows the way out, but not by denial of evil, because it analyses boldly the fact as it is and does not seek to conceal anything. It is not hopeless; it is not agnostic. It finds out a remedy, but it wants to place that remedy on adamantine foundations; not by shutting the child's mouth and blinding its eyes with something which is untrue, and which the child will find out in a few days. I remember when I was young, a young man's father died and left him poorly off, with a large family to support, and he found that his father's friends were unwilling to help him. He had a conversation with a clergyman who offered this consolation, "Oh, it is all good, all is sent for our good." That is the old method of trying to put a piece of gold leaf on an old sore. It is a confession of weakness, of absurdity. The young man went away, and six months afterwards a son was born to the clergyman, and he gave a thanksgiving party to which the young man was invited. The clergyman prayed, "Think God for His mercies," And the young man stood up and said, "Stop, this is all misery." The clergyman asked, "Why?" "Because when my father died you said it was good, though apparently evil ; so now, this is apparently good, but really evil." Is this the way to cure the misery of the world? Be good and have mercy on those who suffer. Do not try to patch it up, nothing will cure this World go beyond it.

This is world of good and evil. Wherever there is good, evil follows, but beyond and behind all these manifestations, all these contradictions, the Vedanta finds out that Unity. It says, "Give up what is evil and give up what is good." What remains then? Behind good and evil stands something which is yours, the real you, beyond every evil, and beyond every good too, and it is that which is manifesting itself as good and bad. Know that first, and then and then alone you will be a true optimist, and not before; for then you will be able to control every thing. Control these manifestations and you will be at liberty to manifest the real "you". First be master of yourself, stand up and be free, go beyond the pale of these laws, for these laws do not absolutely govern you, they are only part of your being. First find out that you are not the slave of nature, never were and never will be; that this nature, infinite as you may think it, is only finite, a drop in the ocean, and your soul is the ocean; you are beyond the stars, the sun, and the moon. They are like mere bubbles compared with your infinite being. Know that, and you will control both good and evil. Then alone the whole vision will change and you will stand up and say, "How beautiful is good and how wonderful is evil!"

That is what the Vedanta teaches. It does not propose any slipshod remedy by covering wounds with gold leaf and the more the wound festers, putting on more gold leaf. This life is a hard fact; work your way through it boldly, though it may be adamantine; no matter, the soul is stronger. It lays no responsibility on little gods; for you are the makers of your own fortunes. You make yourselves suffer, you make good and evil, and it is you who put your hands before your eyes and say it is dark. Take your hands away and see the light; you are effulgent, you are perfect already, from the very beginning. We now understand the verse: "He goes from death to death who sees the many here." See that One and be free.

How are we to see it? This mind, so deluded, so weak, so easily led, even this mind can be strong and may catch a glimpse of that knowledge, that Oneness, which saves us from dying again and again. As rain falling upon a mountain flows in various streams down the sides of the mountain, so all the energies which you see here are from that one Unit. It has become manifold falling upon Maya. Do not run after the manifold; go towards the One. "He is in all that moves; He is in all that is pure; He fills the universe; He is in the sacrifice; He is the guest in the house; He is in man, in water, in animals, in truth; He is the Great One. As fire coming into this world is manifesting itself in various forms, even so, that one Soul of the universe is manifesting himself in all these various forms as air coming into this universe manifests itself in various forms, even so, the One Soul of all souls, of all beings, is manifesting himself in all forms." This is true for you when you have understood this Unity, and not before. Then is all optimism, because He is seen everywhere. The question is that if all this be true that that Pure One the Self, the Infinite—has entered all this, how is it that He suffers, how is it that He becomes miserable, impure? He does not, says the Upanishad. "As the sun is the cause of the eyesight, of every being, yet is not made defective by the defect in any eye, even so the Self of all is not affected by the miseries of the body, or by any misery that is around you." I may have some disease and see everything yellow, but the sun is not affected by it. "He is the One, the Creator of all, the Ruler of all, the Internal Soul of every being He who makes His Oneness manifold. Thus sages who realise Him as the Soul of their souls, unto them belongs eternal peace; unto none else, unto none else. He who in this world of evanescence finds Him who never changes, lie who in this universe of death finds that One Life, he who in this manifold finds that Oneness, and all those who realise Him as the Soul of their souls, to them belongs eternal peace; untonone else, unto none else. Where to find Him in the external world, where to find Him in the suns, and moons, and stars? There the sun cannot illumine, nor the moon, nor the stars, the flash of lightning cannot illumine the place; what to speak of this mortal fire? He shining, everything else shines. It is His light that they have borrowed, and He is shining through them." Here is another beautiful simile. Those of you who have been in India and have seen how the banyan tree comes from one root and spreads itself far around, will understand this. He is that banyan tree; He is the root of all and has branched out until He has become this universe, and however far lie extends, every one of these trunks and branches is connected.

Various heavens are spoken of in the Brahmana portions of the Vedas, but the philosophical teaching of the Upanishads gives up the idea of going to heaven. Happiness is not in this heaven or in that heaven, it is in the soul; places do not signify anything. Here is another passage which shows the different states of realisation "In the heaven of the forefathers, as a man sees things in a dream, so the Real Truth is seen," As in dreams we see things hazy and not so distinct, so we see the reality there. There is another heaven called the *Gandharva*, in which it is still less clear; as a man sees his own reflection in the water, so is the reality seen there. The highest heaven, of which the Hindus conceive is called the Brahmaloka; and in this, the Truth is seen much more clearly, like light and shade, but not yet quite distinctly. But as a man sees his own fare in a mirror, perfect, distinct, and clear, so is the Truth shining in the soul of man. The highest heaven, therefore, is in our own souls; the greatest temple of worship is the human soul, greater than all heavens, says the Vedanta; for in no heaven anywhere, can we understand the reality as distinctly and clearly as in this life, in our own soul. Changing places does not help one much. I thought while I was in India that the cave would give me clearer vision. I found it was not so. Then I thought the forest, would do so, then, Varanasi. But the same difficulty existed everywhere, because we make our own worlds. If I am evil, the whole world is evil to me. That is what the Upanishad says. And the same thing applies to all worlds. If I die and go to heaven, I should find the same, for until I am pure it is no use going to caves, or forests, or to Varanasi, or to heaven, and if I have polished my mirror, it does not matter where I live, I get the Reality just as It is. So it is useless, running hither and thither, and spending energy in vain, which should be spent only in polishing the mirror.

The same idea is expressed again: "None sees Him, none sees His form with the eyes. It is in the mind, in the pure mind, that He is seen, and thus immortality is gained."

Those who were at the summer lectures on Raja-Yoga will be interested to know that what was taught then was a different kind of Yoga. The Yoga which we are now considering consists chiefly in controlling the senses. When the senses are held as slaves by the human soul, when they can no longer disturb the mind, then the Yogi has reached the goal. "When all vain desires of the heart have been given up, then this very mortal becomes immortal, then he becomes one with God even here. When all the knots of the heart are cut asunder, then the mortal becomes immortal, and he enjoys Brahman here." Here, on this earth, nowhere else.

A few words ought to be said here. You will generally hear that this Vedanta, this philosophy and other Eastern systems, look only to something beyond, letting go the enjoyments and struggle of this life. This idea is entirely wrong. It is only ignorant people who do not know anything of Eastern thought, and never had brain enough to understand anything of its real teaching, that tell you so. On the contrary, we read in our scriptures that our philosophers do not want to go to other worlds, but depreciate them as places where people weep and laugh for a little while only, and then die. As long as we are weak we shall have to go through these experiences; but whatever is true, is here, and that is the human soul. And this also is insisted upon, that by committing suicide, we cannot escape the inevitable; we cannot evade it. But the right path is hard to find. The Hindu is just as practical as the Western, only we differ in our views of life. The one says, build a good house, let us have good clothes and food, intellectual culture, and so on, for this is the whole of life; and in that he is immensely practical. But the Hindu says, true knowledge of the world means knowledge of the soul, metaphysics; and he wants to enjoy that life. In America there was a great agnostic, a very noble man, a very good man, and a very fine speaker. He lectured on religion, which he said was of no use; why bother our heads about other worlds? He employed this simile; we have an orange here, and we want to squeeze all the juice out of it. I met him once and said, "I agree with you entirely. I have some fruit, and I too want to squeeze out the juice. Our difference lies in the choice of the fruit. You want an orange, and I prefer a mango. You think it is enough to live here and eat and drink and have a little scientific knowledge; but you have no right to say that that will suit all tastes. Such a conception is nothing to me. If I had only to learn how an apple falls to the ground, or how an electric current shakes my nerves, I would commit suicide. I want to understand the heart of things, the very kernel itself. Your study is the manifestation of life, mine is the life itself. My philosophy says you must know that and drive out from mind all thoughts of heaven and hell and all other superstitions, even though they exist in the same sense that world exists. I must know the heart of this life, its essence, what it is, not only how it works and what its manifestations. I want the why of everything; I leave the how to children. As one of your countrymen 'While I am smoking a cigarette, if I were to write book, it would be the science of the cigarette.' It is and great to be scientific, God bless them in their search; but when a man says that is all, he is talking foolishly not caring to know the raison d'etre of life, never studying existence itself. I may argue that all your knowledge nonsense, without a basis. You are studying the ma festations of life, and when I ask you what life is, you say you do not know. You are welcome to your study, but leave me to mine".

I am practical, very practical, in my own way. So your idea that only the West is practical is nonsense. You are practical in one way, and I in another. There are different types of men and minds. If in the East a man is told that he will find out the truth by standing on one leg all his life. he will pursue that method. If in the West, men hear that there is a gold mine somewhere in an uncivilised country, thousands will face the dangers there, in the hope of getting the gold; and, perhaps, only one succeeds. The same men have heard that they have souls but are content to leave the care of them to the church. The first man will not go near the savages, he says it may be dangerous. But if we tell him that on the top of a high mountain lives a wonderful sage who can give him knowledge of the soul, he tries to climb up to him, even if he is killed in the attempt. Both types of men are practical, but the mistake lies in regarding this world as the whole of life. Yours is the vanishing point of enjoyment of the senses—there is nothing permanent in it, it only brings more and more misery—while mine brings eternal peace.

I do not say your view is wrong, you are welcome to it. Great good and blessing come out of it, but do not, therefore, condemn my view. My view is also practical in its own way. Let us all work on our own plans. All of us are equally practical. I have seen some scientists who were equally practical, both as scientists and as spiritual men, and it is my great hope that in course of time the whole of humanity will be efficient in the same manner. When a kettle of water is coming to the boil, if you watch the phenomenon, you find first one bubble rising, and then another and so on, until at last they all join, and a tremendous commotion takes place. This world is very similar. Each individual is like a bubble, and the nations resemble many bubbles. Gradually these nations join, and I am sure the day will come when separation will vanish and that oneness which we all went will become manifest. A time must come when every man will be as intensely practical in the scientific world as in the spiritual, and then that Oneness, the harmony of Oneness, will pervade the whole world. The whole of mankind will become Jivanmuktas—free whilst living. We are all struggling towards that one end through our jealousies and hatreds, through our love and cooperation. A tremendous stream is flowing towards the ocean carrying us all along with it; and though like straws and scraps of paper we may at times float aimlessly about, in the long run we are sure to join the Ocean of Life and Bliss.

...The Katha Upanishad, which we have been studying, was written much later than that to which we now turn—the Chhandogya. The language is more modern, and the thought more organised. In the older Upanishads the language is very archaic, like that of the hymn portion of the Vedas, and one has to wade sometimes through quite a mass of unnecessary things to get at the essential doctrines. The ritualistic literature about which I told you, which forms the second division of the Vedas, has left a good deal of its mark upon this old Upanishad, so that more than half of it is still ritualistic. There is, however, one great gain in studying the very old Upanishads. You trace, as it were, the historical growth of spiritual ideas. In the more recent Upanishads, the spiritual ideas have been collected and brought into one place; as in the Bhagavad Gita, for instance, which we may, perhaps, look upon as the last of the Upanishads, you do not find any inkling of these ritualistic ideas. The Gita is like a bouquet composed of the beautiful flowers of spiritual truths collected from the Upanishads. But in the Gita you cannot study the rise of the spiritual ideas, you cannot trace them to their source. To do that, as has been pointed out by many, you must study the Vedas. The great idea of holiness that has been attached to these books has preserved them, more than any other book in the world, from mutilation. In them, thoughts at their highest and at their lowest have all been preserved, the essential and the nonessential, the most ennobling teachings and the simplest matters of detail stand side by side; for nobody has dared to touch them. Commentators came and tried to smooth them down and to bring out wonderful new ideas from the old things; they tried to find spiritual ideas in even the most ordinary statements, but the texts remained, and as such, they are the most wonderful historical study. We all know that in the scriptures of every religion changes were made to suit the growing spirituality of later times; one word was changed here and another put in there, and so on. This, probably, has not been done with the Vedic literature, or if ever done, it is almost imperceptible. So we have this great advantage, we are able to study thoughts in their original significance, lo note how they developed, how from materialistic ideas finer and finer spiritual ideas are evolved, until they attained their greatest height in the Vedanta. Descriptions of some of the old manners and customs are also there, but they do not appear much in the Upanishads. The language used is peculiar, terse, mnemonic. The writers of these books simply jotted down these lines as helps to remember certain facts which they supposed were already well known. In a narrative, perhaps, which they are telling, they take it for granted that it is well known to everyone they are addressing. Thus a great difficulty arises, we scarcely know the real meaning of any one of these stories, because the traditions have nearly died out, and the little that is left of them has been very much exaggerated. Many new interpretations have been put upon them, so that when you find them in the Puranas they have already become lyrical poems. Just as in the West, we find this prominent fact in the political development of Western races that they cannot bear absolute rule, that they are always trying to prevent any one man from ruling over them, and are gradually advancing to higher and higher democratic ideas, higher and higher ideas of physical liberty, so, in Indian metaphysics, exactly the same phenomenon appears in the development of spiritual life. The multiplicity of gods gave place to one God of the universe, and in the Upanishads there is a rebellion even against that one God. Not only was the idea of many governors of the universe ruling their destinies unbearable, but it was also intolerable that there should be one person ruling this universe. This is the first thing that strikes us. The idea grows and grows, until it attains its climax. In almost all of the Upanishads, we find the climax coming at the last, and that is the dethroning of this God of the universe. The personality of God vanishes, the impersonality comes. God is no more a person, no more a human being, however magnified and exaggerated, who rules this universe, but He has become an embodied principle in every being, immanent in the whole universe. It would be illogical to go from the Personal God to the Impersonal, and at the same time to leave man as a person. So the personal man is broken down, and man, as principle is built up. The person is only a phenomenon, the principle is behind it. Thus from both sides, simultaneously, we find the breaking down of personalities and the approach towards principles, the Personal God approaching the Impersonal, the personal man approaching the Impersonal Man. Then come the succeeding stages of the gradual convergence of the two advancing lines of the Impersonal God and the Impersonal Man. And the Upanishads embody the stages through which these two lines at last become one, and the last word of each Upanishad is, "Thou art That". There is but One Eternally Blissful Principle, and that One is manifesting Itself as all this variety.

Then came the philosophers. The work of the Upanishads seems to have ended at that point; the next was taken up by the philosophers. The framework was given them by the Upanishads, and they had to fill in the details. So, many questions would naturally arise. Taking for granted that there is but One Impersonal Principle which is manifesting itself in all these manifold forms, how is it that the One becomes many? It is another way of putting the same old question which in its crude form comes into the human heart as the inquiry into the cause of evil and so forth. Why does evil exist in the world, and what is its cause? But the same question has now become refined, abstracted. No more is it asked from the platform of the senses why we are unhappy, but from the platform of philosophy. How is it that this One Principle becomes manifold? And the answer, as we have seen, the best answer that India has produced is the theory of Maya which says that It really has not become manifold, that It really has not lost any of its real nature. Manifoldness is only apparent. Man is only apparently a person, but in reality he is the Impersonal Being. God is a person only apparently, but really He is the Impersonal Being.

Even in this answer there have been succeeding stages, and philosophers have varied in their opinions. All Indian philosophers did not admit this theory of Maya. Possibly most of them did not. There are dualists, with a crude sort of dualism, who would not allow the question to be asked, but stifled it at its very birth. They said, "You have no right to ask such a question, you have no right to ask for an explanation; it is simply the will of God, and we have to submit to it quietly. There is no liberty for the human soul. Everything is predestined what we shall do, have, enjoy, and suffer; and when suffering comes, it is our duty to endure it patiently; if we do not, we shall be punished all the more. How do we know that? Because the Vedas say so." And thus they have their texts and their meanings and they want to enforce them.

There are others who, though not admitting the Maya theory, stand midway. They say that the whole of this creation forms, as it were, the body of God. God is the Soul of all souls and of the whole of nature. In the case of individual souls, contraction comes from evil doing. When a man does anything evil, his soul begins to contract and his power is diminished and goes on decreasing, until he does good works, when it expands again. One idea seems to be common in all the Indian systems, and I think, in every system in the world, whether they know it or not, and that is what I should call the divinity of man. There is no one system in the world, no real religion, which does not hold the idea that the human soul, whatever it be, or whatever its relation to God, is essentially pure and perfect, whether expressed in the language of mythology, allegory, or philosophy. Its real nature is blessedness and power, not weakness and misery. Somehow or other this misery has come. The crude systems may call it a personified evil, a devil or an Ahriman, to explain how this misery came. Other systems may try to make a God and a devil in one, who makes some people miserable and others happy, without any reason whatever. Others again, more thoughtful, bring in the theory of Maya and so forth. But one fact stands out clearly, and it is with this that we have to deal. After all, these philosophical ideas and systems are but gymnastics of the mind, intellectual exercises. The one great idea that to me seems to be clear, and comes out through masses of superstition in every country and in every religion, is the one luminous idea that man is divine, that divinity is our nature.

Whatever else comes is a mere superimposition, as the Vedanta calls it. Something has been superimposed, but that divine nature never dies. In the most degraded as well as in the most saintly it is ever present. It has to be called out, and it will work itself out. We have to ask, and it will manifest itself. The people of old knew, that fire lived in the flint and in dry wood, but friction was necessary to call it out. So this fire of freedom and purity is the nature of every soul, and not a quality, because qualities can be acquired and therefore can be lost. The soul is one with Freedom, and the soul is one with Existence, and the soul is one with Knowledge. The Sat-Chit-Ananda—Existence-Knowledge-Bliss Absolute—is the nature, the birthright of the Soul, and all the manifestations that we see are Its expressions, dimly or brightly manifesting Itself. Even death is but a manifestation of that Real Existence. Birth and death, life and decay, degeneration and regeneration—are all manifestations of that Oneness. So, knowledge, however it manifests itself, either as ignorance or as learning, is but the manifestation of that same Chit, the essence of knowledge; the difference is only in degree, and not in kind. The difference in knowledge between the lowest worm that crawls under our feet and the highest genius that the world may produce is only one of degree, and not of kind. The Vedantin thinker boldly says that the enjoyments in this life, even the most degraded joys, are but manifestations of that One Divine Bliss, the Essence of the Soul.

This idea seems to be the most prominent in Vedanta, and, as I have said, it appears to me that every religion holds it. I have yet to know the religion which does not. It is the one universal idea working through all religions. Take the Bible for instance. You find there the allegorical statement that the first man Adam was pure, and that his purity was obliterated by his evil deeds afterwards. It is clear from this allegory that they thought that the nature of the primitive man was perfect. The impurities that we see, the weaknesses that we feel, are but superimpositions on that nature, and the subsequent history of the Christian religion shows that they also believe in the possibility, nay, the certainty of regaining that old state. This is the whole history of the Bible, Old and New Testaments together. So with the Mohammedans: they also believed in Adam and the purity of Adam, and through Mohammed the way was, opened to regain that lost state. So with the Buddhists: they believe in the state called Nirvana which is beyond this relative world.

It is exactly the same as the Brahman of the Vedantins and the whole system of the Buddhists is founded upon the idea of regaining that lost state of Nirvana. In every system we find this doctrine present, that you cannot get anything which is not yours already. You are indebted to nobody in this universe. You claim your own birthright, as it has been most poetically expressed by a great Vedantin philosopher, in the title of one of his books— "The attainment of our own empire". That empire is ours; we have lost it and we have to regain it. The Mayavadin, however, says that this losing of the empire was a hallucination; you never lost it. This is the only difference.

Although all the systems agree so far that we had the empire, and that we have lost it, they give us varied advice as to how to regain it. One says that you must perform certain ceremonies, pay certain sums of money to certain idols, eat certain sorts of food, live in a peculiar fashion to regain that empire. Another says that if you weep and prostrate yourselves and ask pardon of some Being beyond nature, you will regain that empire. Again, another says if you love such a Being with all your heart, you will regain that empire. All this varied advice is in the Upanishads. As I go on, you will find it so. But the last and the greatest counsel is that you need not weep at all. You need not go through all these ceremonies, and need not take any notice of how to regain your empire, because you never lost it. Why should you go to seek for what you never lost? You are pure already, you are free already. If you think you are free, free you are this moment, and if you think you are bound, bound you will be. This is a very bold statement, and as I told you at the beginning of this course, I shall have to speak to you very boldly. It may frighten you now, but when you think over it, and realise it in your own life, then you will come to know that what I say is true. For, supposing that freedom is not your nature, by no manner of means can you become free. Supposing you were free and in some way you lost that freedom, that shows that you were not free to begin with. Had you been free, what could have made you lose it? The independent can never be made dependent; if it is really dependent, its independence was a hallucination.

Of the two sides, then, which will you take? If you say that the soul was by its own nature pure and free, it naturally follows that there was nothing in this universe which could make it bound or limited. But if there was anything in nature which could bind the soul, it naturally follows that it was not free, and your statement that it was free is a delusion. So if it is possible for us to attain to freedom, the conclusion is inevitable that the soul is by its nature free. It cannot be otherwise. Freedom means independence of anything outside, and that means that nothing outside itself could work upon it as a cause. The soul is causeless, and from this follow all the great ideas that we have. You cannot establish the immortality of the soul, unless you grant that it is by its nature free, or in other words, that it cannot be acted upon by anything outside. For death is an effect produced by some outside cause. I drink poison and I die, thus showing that my body can be acted upon by something outside that is called poison. But if it be true that the soul is free, it naturally follows that nothing can affect it, and it can never die. Freedom, immortality, blessedness, all depend upon the soul being beyond the law of causation, beyond this Maya. Of these two which will you take? Either make the first a delusion, or make the second a delusion. Certainly I will make the second a delusion. It is more consonant with all my feelings and aspirations. I am perfectly aware that I am free by nature, and I will not admit that this bondage is true and my freedom a delusion.

This discussion goes on in all philosophies, in some form or other. Even in the most modern philosophies you find the same discussion arising. There are two parties. One says that there is no soul, that the idea of soul is a delusion produced by the repeated transit of particles of matter, bringing about the combination which you call the body or the brain; that the impression of freedom is the result of the vibrations and motions and continuous transit of these particles. There were Buddhistic sects who held the same view and illustrated it by this example: If you take a torch and whirl it round rapidly, there will be a circle of light. That circle does not really exist, because the torch is changing place every moment. We are but bundles of little particles, which in their rapid whirling produce the delusion of a permanent soul. The other party states that in the rapid succession of thought, matter occurs as a delusion, and does not really exist. So we see one side claiming that spirit is a delusion and the other, that matter is a delusion. Which side will you take? Of course, we will take the spirit and deny matter. The arguments are similar for both, only on the spirit side the argument is little stronger. For nobody has ever seen what matter is. We can only feel ourselves. I never knew a man who could feel matter outside of himself. Nobody was ever able to jump outside of himself. Therefore the argument is a little stronger on the side of the spirit. Secondly, the spirit theory explains the universe, while materialism does not. Hence the materialistic explanation is illogical. If you boil down all the philosophies and analyse them, you will find that they are reduced to one or the other of these two positions. So here, too, in a more intricate form, in a more philosophical form, we find the same question about natural purity and freedom. One side says that the first is a delusion, and the other, that the second is a delusion. And, of course, we side with the second, in believing that our bondage is a delusion.

The solution of the Vedanta is that we are not bound, we are free already. Not only so, but to say or to think that we are bound is dangerous—it is a mistake, it is selfhypnotism. As soon as you say, "I am bound", "I am weak", "I am helpless" woe unto you; you rivet one more chain upon yourself. Do not say it, do not think it. I have heard of a man who lived in a forest and used to repeat day and night, "Shivoham"—I am the Blessed One—and one day a tiger fell upon him and dragged him away to kill him; people on the other side of the river saw it, and heard the voice so long as voice remained in him, saying, "Shivoham"—even in the very jaws of the tiger. There have been many such men. There have been cases of men who, while being cut to pieces, have blessed their enemies. "I am He, I am He; and so art thou. I am pure and perfect and so are all my enemies. You are He, and so am I". That is the position of strength. Nevertheless, there are great and wonderful things in the religions of the dualists; wonderful is the idea of the Personal God apart from nature, whom we worship and love. Sometimes this idea is very soothing. Hut, says The Vedanta says that the soothing is something like the effect that comes from an opiate which is not natural. It brings weakness in the long run, and what this world wants today, more than it ever did before, is strength. It is weakness, says the Vedanta, which is the cause of all misery in this world. Weakness is the one cause of suffering. We become miserable because we are weak. We lie, steal, kill, and commit other crimes, because we are weak. We suffer because we are weak. We die because we are weak. Where there is nothing to weaken us, there is neither death nor sorrow. We are miserable through delusion. Give up the delusion, and the whole thing vanishes. It is plain and simple indeed. Through all these philosophical discussions and tremendous mental gymnastics, we come to this one religious idea, the simplest in the whole world.

The monistic Vedanta is the simplest form in which you can put the truth. To teach dualism was a tremendous mistake made in India and elsewhere, because people did not look at the ultimate principles, but only thought of the process which is very intricate indeed. To many, these tremendous philosophical and logical propositions were alarming. They thought these things could not be made universal, could not be followed in everyday practical life, and that under the guise of such a philosophy, the much laxity of living would arise.

But I do not believe at all that monistic ideas preached to the world would produce immorality and weakness. On the contrary, I have reason to believe that it is the only remedy. If this be the truth, why let people drink ditch water when the stream of life is flowing nearby? If this be the truth, that they are all pure, why not at this moment teach it to the whole world? Why not teach it with the voice of thunder to every man that is born, to saints and sinners, men, women, and children, to the man on the throne and to the man sweeping the streets?

It appears now a very big and a very great undertaking; to many it appears very startling, but that is because of superstition, nothing else. By eating all sorts of bad and indigestible food, or by starving ourselves, we are incompetent to eat a good meal. We have listened to words of weakness from our childhood. You hear people say that they do not believe in ghosts, but at the same time, there are very few who do not get a little creepy sensation in the dark. It is simply superstition. So with all religious superstitions. There are people in this country who, if I told them there was no such being as the devil, will think all religion is gone. Many people have said to me, how can there be religion without a devil? How can there be religion without someone to direct us? How can we live without being ruled by somebody? We like to be so treated, because we have become used to it. We are not happy until we feel we have been reprimanded by somebody every day. The same superstition! But however terrible it may seem now, the time will come when we shall look back, each one of us, and smile at every one of those superstitions which covered the pure and eternal soul, and repeat with gladness, with truth, and with strength, I am free, and was free, and always will be free. This monistic idea will come out of Vedanta, and it is the one idea that deserves to live. The scriptures may perish tomorrow. Whether this idea first flashed into the brains of Hebrews or of people living in the Arctic regions, nobody cares. For this is the truth and truth is eternal; and truth itself teaches that it is not the special property of any individual or nation. Men, animals, and gods are all common recipients of this one truth. Let them all receive it. Why make life miserable? Why let people fall into all sorts of superstitions? I will give ten thousand lives, if twenty of them will give up their superstition. Not only in this country, but in the land of its very birth, if you tell people this truth, they are frightened. They say, "This idea is for Sannyasins who give up the world and live in forests; for them it is all right. But for us poor householders, we must all have some sort of fear, we must have ceremonies," and so on.

Dualistic ideas have ruled the world long enough, and this is the result. Why not make a new experiment? It may take ages for all minds to receive monism, but why not begin now? If we have told it to twenty persons in our lives, we have done a great work.

There is one idea which often militates against it. It is this. It is all very well to say, "I am the Pure, the Blessed", but I cannot show it always in my life. That is true; the ideal is always very hard. Every child that is born sees the sky overhead very far away, but is that any reason why we should not look towards the sky? Would it mend matters to go towards superstition? If we cannot get nectar, would it mend matters for us to drink poison? Would it be any help for us, because we cannot realise the truth immediately, to go into darkness and yield to weakness and superstition?

I have no objection to dualism in many of its forms, I like most of them, but I have objections to every form of teaching which inculcates weakness. This is the one question I put to every man, woman, or child, when they are in physical, mental, or spiritual training. Are you strong? Do you feel strength?—for I know it is truth alone that gives strength. I know that truth alone gives life, and nothing but going towards reality will make us strong, and none will reach truth until he is strong. Every system, therefore, which weakens the mind, makes one superstitious, makes one mope, makes one desire all sorts of wild impossibilities, mysteries, and superstitions, I do not like, because its effect is dangerous. Such systems never bring any good; such things create morbidity in the mind, make it weak, so weak that in course of time it will be almost impossible to receive truth or live up to it. Strength, therefore, is the one thing needful. Strength is the medicine for the world's disease. Strength is the medicine which the poor must have when tyrannised over by the rich. Strength is the medicine that the ignorant must have when oppressed by the learned; and it is the medicine that sinners must have when tyrannised over by other sinners; and nothing gives such strength as this idea of monism. Nothing makes us so moral as this idea of monism.

Nothing makes us work so well at our best and highest as when all the responsibility is thrown upon ourselves. I challenge everyone of you. How will you behave if I put a little baby in your hands? Your whole life will be changed for the moment; whatever you may be, you must become selfless for the time being. You will give up all your criminal ideas as soon as responsibility is thrown upon you—your whole character will change. So if the whole responsibility is thrown upon our own shoulders, we shall be at our highest and best; when we have nobody to grope forwards, no devil to lay our blame upon, no Personal God to carry our burdens, when we are alone responsible, then we shall rise to our highest and best. I am responsible for my fate, I am the bringer of good unto myself, I am the bringer of evil. I am the Pure and Blessed One. We must reject all thoughts that assert the contrary. "I have neither death nor fear, I have neither caste nor creed, I have neither father nor mother nor brother, neither friend nor foe, for I am Existence, Knowledge, and Bliss Absolute; I am the Blissful One, I am the Blissful One. I am not bound either by virtue or vice, by happiness or misery. Pilgrimages and books and ceremonials can never bind me. I have neither hunger nor thirst; the body is not mine, nor am I subject to the superstitions and decay that come to the body, I am Existence, Knowledge, and Bliss Absolute; I am the Blissful One, I am the Blissful One.

This, says the Vedanta, is the only prayer that we should have. This is the only way to reach the goal, to tell ourselves, and to tell everybody else, that we are divine. And as we go on repeating this, strength comes. He who falters at first will get stronger and stronger, and the voice will increase in volume until the truth takes possession of our hearts, and courses through our veins, and permeates our bodies. Delusion will vanish as the light becomes more and more effulgent, load after load of ignorance will vanish, and then will come a time when all else has disappeared and the sun alone shines.

2

Collection from the Complete Works of Swami Abhedananda

...... CENTURIES before the Christian era, nay, long before the advent of the prophet and founder of Judaism, when the forefathers of the Anglo-Saxon races were living in caves and forests, tattooing their bodies, eating raw animal flesh, wearing animal skins,—in that remote antiquity, the dawn of true civilisation broke upon the horizon of India, or Bharata Varsha, as it is called in Sanskrit.

The ancient Vedic sages had already perfected their lofty system of moral philosophy, and their followers were well-established in the practice of the ethical and spiritual teachings of the Vedas even before Moses* had reformed the lawless and nomadic tribes of Israel by giving them the ten commandments in the name of Jahveh. And while thinkers among the Semitic tribes were still trying to explain the origin of the human race and of the universe through the mythological stories of creation collected from the Chaldeans, Phoenicians, Babylonians and Persians, the Aryan philosophers of India had already discovered the evolution of the universe out of one eternal Energy, and of man from the lower animals.

Many people have an idea that India is inhabited by idolatrous heathens, who have neither philosophy, ethics, science, nor religion, and that whatever they possess they have acquired from the Christian missionaries: but, since the Parliament of Religions at the World's Fair in Chicago in 1893, the educated men and women of this country have - cast aside all such erroneous notions. They have learned, on the contrary, that India has always been the fountain-head of every system of philosophy, and the home of all the religious thought of the world. The majority of Oriental scholars, like Professor Max Mtiller and Professor Paul Deussen, as also advanced students in America, have now come to realise that from ancient times India has produced a nation of philosophers, and that all the phases of philosophic thought, whether ancient or modern, can still be found there today". Victor Cousin, the eminent French philosopher, whose knowledge of the history of European philosophy was unrivalled, writes: "When we read the poetical and philosophical monuments of the East,—above all, those of India, which are beginning to spread in Europe, —we discover there many a truth, and truths so profound, and which make such a contrast with the meanness of the results at which the European genius has sometimes stopped, that we are constrained to bend the knee before the philosophy of the East, and to see in this cradle of the human race the native land of the highest philosophy." *And elsewhere he declares that "India contains the whole history of philosophy in a nutshell."

You will find no other country in the world where, from prehistoric times down to the present day, philosophy and religion have played so important a part in forming the character of the nation as they have done in India. India is the only country where, at least two thousand years before the Christian era, public assemblies, philosophic conventions, and religious congresses were held under the auspices of the reigning monarchs; and in these active part was taken, not only by priests, philosophers, and scientists, but by kings, military commanders, soldiers, merchants, peasants, and educated women of the higher classes. As early as the Vedic period, which dates from 5000 to 2000 B.C., the ancient Seers of Truth asked the most vital questions, and discussed problems that have troubled the minds of the great philosophers of all ages.

In those questions we can discern the development of their intellectual powers, and their insight into the true nature of things. They inquired: "When death swallows the whole world, who is the deity which shall swallow death? What part of man exists after death? What becomes of the vital forces when a man dies? What is the nature of the soul? Where is the foundation and support of this universe? What' is the essence of being? What is there that governs all things and yet is separate from everything?' In trying to answer these and other problems of similar nature, the ancient thinkers discovered the laws of thought and traced the causes of phenomena, applying the rules of logic and reason at every step.

This was the beginning of philosophy in India. The minds of those truthseekers were absolutely free from all limitations of doctrines, dogmas, and creeds. They never asked what their belief was, or whether they had faith in a personal God; but the burning questions for them were, how to acquire true knowledge of the universe, of its origin and cause, how to know the real nature of their souls, and how to solve the problems of life and death. At that time philosophic and religious thought began to ferment as actively and universally in the atmosphere of India as we find to-day in Western countries. Some of the answers given to these questions by the unbiassed thinkers of those days are truly astounding; it seems as though the ancient Seers of Truth had anticipated the conclusions of Plato, Spinoza, Berkeley, Hume, Hegel, Schopenhauer, Herbert Spencer, Haeckel, even centuries before their existence.

During the pre-Buddhistic period, or before the sixth century B.C., India gave rise to a great variety of philosophical systems, some of which were atheistic, agnostic, nihilistic, materialistic, while others were pluralistic, dualistic, or monotheistic, qualified nondualistic, idealistic, spiritualistic, monistic systems of thought, such as are common in Europe and America at the present time. In fact, the natural tendency of the Hindu mind from the very beginning was to search after the unchangeable Reality of the universe, to trace the source of all phenomena, to understand the purpose of earthly existence, and, above all, to know what relation the individual soul bears to the Universal Being. Animated by an intense longing and guided by unswerving love for Truth, the ancient thinkers discovered many of the natural laws, and rationally explained them, without fearing contradiction or persecution; for freedom of thought has always prevailed among all classes of people in India.

These sages understood the process of cosmic, evolution from a homogeneous mass into the variety of phenomena, and rejected the theory of special creation out of nothing. In one of, the Upanishads we read that a sage, after explaining the mystery of Creation to his son, said: "My dear child, some people think that this world has come out of nothing, but how can something come out of nothing?" Thus we see that, unlike, the Hebrews, the Hindu thinkers did not believe in special creation, but from ancient times maintained the theory of gradual evolution. It has often been remarked that the doctrine of evolution is the marvel of modern times, and that it was unknown in the past ages, but the students of Oriental literature are well aware that it was well known to the Hindus of the Vedic ages. Professor Huxley admits this when he says: "To say nothing of Indian sages, to whom evolution was a familiar notion ages before Paul of Tarsus was born." And Sir Monier Monier Williams, in his "Brahminism and Hinduism, declares: "Indeed, if I may be allowed the anachronism, the Hindus were Spinozites more than two thousand years before the existence of Spinoza; and Darwinians" many centuries before Darwin; and evolutionists many centuries before the doctrine of evolution had been accepted by the scientists of our time, and before any word like 'evolution' existed in any language of the world." This statement is absolutely correct. If we study the philosophical systems of the great thinkers and Seers of Truth of ancient India, we shall find the most wonderful discoveries that have ever been recorded in the whole history of philosophy.

In their attempts to solve the mysteries of the phenomenal world, Hindu Seers of Truth developed six principal systems of philosophy, each having numerous branches of its own. One school traces the origin of the universe to the combination of atoms and molecules. It is known as the Vaisheshika philosophy of Kanada. The system of Kanada divides the phenomenal universe into six Padarthas, or categories, which embrace the whole realm of knowledge. They are these: (1) Dravya, or substance; (2) Guna, or quality; (3) Karma, or action; (4) Samavaya, or that which constitutes a genus; (5) Vishesha, or that which constitutes the individuality or separateness of an object; and (6) Samavaya, coherence or inseparability. According to some, Abhava, or non-existence, is the seventh substance.

Each of these, again, is subdivided into various classes. There are, for instance, nine substances: (1) earth; (2) water; (3) light; (4) air; (5) ether; (6) time (Kala); (7) space (Dish); (8) self (Atman); and (9) mind (Manas). These substances, again, cannot exist without qualities, of which there are seventeen:-colour, taste, smell, touch, number (that by which we perceive one or many); extension or quantity, individuality, conjunction, priority, posteriority, thought, pleasure, pain, desire, aversion, and will. The substances are affected by five kinds of action: (1) upward motion, (2) downward motion, (3) contraction, (4) expansion, (5) movement from one spot to another. All the objects of knowledge must be either substance, quality, or motion.

According to Kanada, the first four substances are non-eternal as aggregates, but are made up of minute invisible atoms (anus) which are eternal. They exist as inorganic and organic matter, or as instruments of sense-perceptions. Kanada describes atoms (anus) as indivisible particles of matter which possess-no visible-dimensions. On this point he agrees more with modern European scientists than with Greek philosophers, who gave visible dimensions to atoms. The first aggregate of these atoms is of two (anus). It is called Dyanu, or molecule, which is still invisible. The aggregate of three molecules or double atoms forms a *Trasarenu*, which has visible dimension. These aggregates of composite atoms are destructible, while single atoms are indestructible by nature. How remarkable it is to see that the conception of atoms and molecules arose in India centuries before the time of Empedocles and Democritus! And the latest atomic theory of European science has not in any way surpassed that of ancient India.

Furthermore, the Vaisheshika system maintains that these atoms are not created by God, but are coeternal with Him. The power, however, which combines two atoms and makes aggregates of atoms, comes from God, who is personal, who possesses knowledge, desire, and will, and who is the one Lord and Governor of all phenomena. According to this system, ether, time, space, Atman or Self, and mind or Manas, are eternal substances of nature. Mind or Manas is described as infinitely small, like an atom (anus); but it is distinct from Atman or Self, which is vast (Vibhu). Although mind and Atman or Self are eternal, still they are innumerable. The Self or Atman is distinct from the senses, and possesses nine qualities, such as knowledge, will, desire, happiness, etc. The aim of the Vaisheshika philosophy (which derives its name from Vishesha, the fifth substance) is the attainment of perfection and absolute freedom of the soul through the right knowledge of the causes of the phenomenal universe.

Next to the Vaisheshika is the Nyaya philosophy of Gautama. Although it is generally called a system of logic, still it is both logic and philosophy. Its object is the same as other Hindu systems, namely, the true knowledge of nature, soul and God, and the attainment of ultimate freedom. This system, although based upon the atomic theory of Kanada, begins with the enumeration of sixteen Padarthas, or subjects for discussion: (1) Pramana, proof or means of knowledge; (2) Prameya, or objects of knowledge; (3) Sansaya, or doubt; (4) Prayojana, motive or purpose; (5) Dristanta, example or instance; (6) Siddhanta, or determined truth; (7) Avayava, syllogism or premises; (8) Tarka, reasoning or confutation; (9) Nirnaya, or conclusion; (10) Vada, or argumentation; (11) Jalpa, or sophistry; (12) Vitanda, objection; (13) Hetvabhdsa, or fallacies; (14) Chhala, quibble or perversion; (15) Jati, or false analogies; and, (16) Nigrahasthana, or unfitness for arguing. The correct knowledge of each of these is the aim of this school. According to Gautama, the means of knowledge are four: (1) sensuous perception; (2) inference; (3) analogy; (4) Shabda, or verbal testimony.

The objects of knowledge are twelve in number Self or Atman, body, organs of senses, objective perception, intellect (Buddhi), mind (Manas), will, fault, state after death, retribution, pain, and final emancipation. These objects, as well as the means of knowledge, which are described singly and elaborately, form the fundamental principles of the philosophy of Nyaya, while the rest of the Padarthas belong to the system of logic which it expounds. Therefore it is both logic and philosophy. Gautama is called the Aristotle of India. He was the founder of Hindu logic, which has gradually developed into a perfect logical system, and to which have been added voluminous works by the best Hindu logicians of later date. The principal aim of Gautama's system was to establish right methods of reasoning, and to develop correct inference by the construction of true syllogisms. The Hindu syllogism consists of five parts: (1) proposition, (2) reason, (3) instance, (4) application of the reason, and (5) conclusion. By omitting two parts of this, we can make it a perfect syllogism of Aristotle. The connection in the major premises of Aristotle's syllogism is called 'in Hindu logic Vyapti, or invariable concomitance. Speaking of Hindu logic, Mr. Davies says: "The right methods of reasoning have been discussed with as much subtlety as by any of the Western logicians." Many European scholars, after finding a close resemblance between the logic of Aristotle and that of Gautama, have arrived at the conclusion that perhaps the Greeks borrowed the first elements of their logic and philosophy from the Hindus. Mr. Dutt says: "Comparing dates, we are disposed to say of this as of many other sciences, The Hindus invented logic, the Greeks perfected it." We must not forget the historical fact that there was a close intercourse between the Greeks and the Hindus from the time of Pythagoras, who, it is said, went to India to gather the wisdom of the Hindus. Alexander himself was so deeply impressed, when he heard about the Hindu philosophers, that he desired to make their acquaintance. It is also said that he brought many Hindu philosophers back to Greece with him. These two schools of philosophy, the Vaisheshika and the Nyaya, supplement each other, and have at present many followers in some parts of India, especially in Bengal and among the Jains.

Then comes the Sankhya system of Kapila. Kapila lived about 700 B.C. He is called the father of the evolution theory in India. His system is more like the philosophy of Herbert Spencer. He rejected the atomic theory by tracing the origin of atoms to one eternal cosmic energy, which he called Prakriti (Latin, Procreatrix, the creative energy). He maintained that the whole phenomenal universe has evolved out of one cosmic energy which is eternal. Kapila defined atoms as force centers, which correspond to the Ions and Electrons of modern science. It was Kapila who for the first time explained creation as the result of attraction and repulsion, which literally means love and hatred of atoms, as Empedocles puts it.

The Sankya philosophy of Kapila, in short, is devoted entirely to the systematic, logical, and scientific explanation of the process of cosmic evolution from that primordial Prakriti, or eternal Energy. There is no ancient philosophy in the world which was not indebted to the Sankhya system of Kapila. The idea of evolution which the ancient Greeks and neo-Platonists had can be traced back to the influence of this Sankhya school of thought. Professor E.W. Hopkins says "Plato is full of Sankhyan thought, worked out by him, but taken from Pythagoras. Before the sixth century B.C. all the religious-philosophical ideas of Pythagoras are current in India (L. Schroeder, Pythagoras). If there were but one or two of these cases, they might be set aside as accidental coincidences, but such coincidences are too numerous to be the result of chance." And again he writes: "Neo-Platonism and Christian-Gnosticism owe much to India". The Gnostic Ideas in regard to a plurality of heavens and spiritual worlds go back directly to Hindu sources. Soul and light are one in the Sankhya system, before they became so in Greece, and when they appear united in Greece it is by means of the thought which is borrowed from India. The famous three qualities of the Sankhya reappear as the Gnostic 'three classes'.

In his "Hindu Philosophy, John Davies speaks of Kapila's system as the first recorded system of philosophy in the world, and calls it" "the earliest attempt on record to give an answer, from reason alone, to the mysterious questions which arise in every thoughtful mind about the origin of the world, the nature and relations of man and his future destiny." Furthermore, Mr. Davies says, in reference to the German philosophy of Schopenhauer and of Hartmann, that it is "a reproduction of the philosophic system of Kapila in its materialistic part, presented in a more elaborate form, but on the same fundamental lines. In this respect the human intellect' has gone over the same ground that it occupied more than two thousand years ago; but on a more important question it has taken a step in retreat. Kapila recognised fully the existence of a soul in man, forming indeed his proper nature,—the absolute of Fichte,—distinct from matter and immortal; but our latest philosophy, both here and in Germany, can see in man only a highly developed organization."

It is most startling to find that the ultimate conclusions of this Sankhya system harmonize and coincide with those of modern science. It says: (1) Something cannot come out of nothing; (2) The effect lies in the cause, that is, the effect is the cause reproduced; (3) Destruction means the reversion of an effect to its causal state; (4) The laws of nature are uniform and regular throughout; (5) The building up of the cosmos is the result of the evolution of the cosmic energy. These are some of the conclusions which Kapila arrived at through observation and experiment, and by following strictly the rules of inductive logic, Kapila denied the existence of a Creator; but still his philosophy is not considered atheistic, because he admitted the existence of the individual soul, Purusha, as an eternal and immortal entity. The different schools of Buddhistic philosophy are based upon the Sankhya system, of Kapila. The gnosticism of the Jain philosopliy, which has now a large number of followers in India, is also based upon the truths "of this system; while the main principles of the *Sakhya* teachings have played a most important" part in the popular forms of the symbol-worship of modern India.

Next in order comes the Yoga philosophy of Patanjali. Patanjali accepts the theory of evolution as explained by Kapila, and maintains that the whole phenomenal universe is the result of the evolution of Prakriti, the eternal Energy. Like Kapila, Patanjali believes in the existence of countless Purushas, or individual souls, each of which is by nature eternal, infinite, and immortal. But this system differs from Sankhya by admitting the existence of a cosmic Purusha (personal God), who is formless, infinite, omniscient, and untouched by affliction, activity, deserts, and desires. Patanjali takes up the psychology of Sankhya, and explains most elaborately the various functions of the Chitta, or mind substance. Both Kapila and Patanjali maintain that mind substance is material,—that it is the product of the insentient Prakriti. On this point they anticipated the conclusions of the materialistic philosophers of modern Europe; but they admitted that mind substance, or Chitta, is distinct from Purusha, or true Self, which is the source of consciousness and intelligence.

The Yoga system devotes itself to the higher psychology of the human mind. It divides Chitta into five classes of Vrittis, or modifications: right knowledge, indiscrimination, verbal delusion, sleep, memory. Right knowledge proceeds from direct sensuous perception, inference, and competent evidence. These and various other mental functions are minutely described by Patanjali after explaining all the modifications of the Chitta, Patanjali shows the method by which absolute control over mind (Manas), intellect (Buddhi). Chitta, and egotism (Ahankara) can be attained. For the highest aim of his philosophy is to separate the Purusha from Prakriti, with which it is at present closely related; and make it reach Kaivalya, or final emancipation the bondage of nature and its qualities. Patanjali also explains the science of concentration and meditation, the science of breath, clairaudience, telepathy, and various other psychic powers, and shows the way by which one can attain to God-consciousness in this life. There is no system of psychological philosophy in the world so complete as the psychology of Patanjali. The modern psychology of Europe, strictly speaking, is not true psychology, because it does not admit the existence of Psyche, the soul; Schopenhauer says: "The study of psychology is vain, for there is no Psyche." It may be called physiological psychology, or sometology, at my friend, Professor Hiram Corson, of Cornell University, calls it. True psychology you will find today in the Yoga system of Patanjali this philosophy has still many followers in different parts of India.

There is yet another school of philosophy called the *Purva Mimansa* of *Jaimini*. The word "*Mimansa*" means investigation, and "Purva" means former or prior. This system examines the various injunctions of the ritualistic portion of the Vedas (Karma Kanda), and points out that the highest duty of man is to follow those injunctions as strictly as possible, for they are the direct revelation of the Supreme Being. According to Jaimini, the words of the Vedas are eternal, and the relation of these words to their meaning is also eternal; so the Vedas had no human origin. This system of philosophy explains the authoritative sources of knowledge, the relation between word and thought, and how this world is the manifestation of the word. We see a cow because there is in the Vedas such a word as "cow" (in the Sanskrit Gau). If the word cow did not exist, the material object as cow would, be nonexistent. We may laugh at such conclusions at present, but when go deep into the subject and try to understand the relation which lies between thought and word, we shall realise the truth of such statements. The sun exists because there is the word "sun" in the Vedas; that is, the sun is nothing but a part of the manifestation of that Logos or eternal thought form which exists in the cosmic mind.

Purva Mimansa may also be called the philosophy of work. It describes the true nature duty and of daily works, sacrificial, ritualistic, and devotional. Through it we can understand which is right work and in what way it should be performed to produce certain results. For instance, if we wish to go to heaven we shall have to perform certain acts and those acts will create a certain unknown or imperceptible result, which will be rewarded or manifested in the form of our going to heaven. Now, how do these things happen? What is the law? And if we perform that very act in some other way, what defects would be produced in the result? All these minute points are discussed. You may throw them away as speculation, but those who believe in the efficacy of prayers, in the law of action and reaction, of cause and sequence, cannot reject them as mere speculation, because there is some truth in them. We cannot deny it. Every thought that we think or every movement of the body that we make, must produce some result somewhere in some form. What are those results? How will they affect our being? We are too busy to think of these subtle problems now, but there are thinkers who can explain a great deal on these higher and finer lines of nature. Referring to the logic of this system, Professor Colebrook says: "Each case is examined and determined upon general principles, and from the cases decided the principles may be collected. A well ordered arrangement, of them would constitute the philosophy of law; and this is, in truth, what has been attempted in the Mimansa." This being an orthodox philosophy, it appeals to the students of the Vedas, and especially to the Brahmin priests.

Lastly comes the Uttara Mimansa, or the system of Vedanta. This is the most popular philosophy of India today. Since the decline of Buddhistic philosophy in India, Vedanta has become most prominent and most powerful, having a large following among all classes of people, from the priests down to the pariahs. Among the six schools, the Vedanta philosophy has reached the highest pinnacle of philosophic thought which the human mind can possibly attain. A careful study of these different systems shows that they contain all the highest truths which were known to the ancient Greek philosophers of the Pythagorean and Eleatic schools. Professor E. W. Hopkins says: "Both Thales and Parmenides were indeed anticipated by Hindu sages, and the Eleatic school seems to be but a reflection of the Upanishads". The doctrines of Anaxamander and Heraclitus were perhaps not known first in Greece. Frederic Schlegel writes: "The divine origin of man, as taught" by the Vedanta, is continually inculcated, to stimulate his efforts to return, to animate him in the struggle, and incite him to consider a reunion and reincorporation with Divinity as the one primary object of every action and reaction. Even the loftiest philosophy of the Europeans, the idealism of reason as it is set forth by the Greek philosophers, appears in comparison with the abundant light and vigor of Oriental idealism like a feeble Promethean spark in the 'full flood of heavenly glory of the noonday sun, faltering and feeble and ever ready to be extinguished. The ultimate reality of the universe, according to Vedanta, is the one Absolute Substance which is beyond subject and object, which is the infinite source of intelligence or knowledge, of consciousness and blissfulness, which is one and not many. It is called in Sanskrit Brahman. It is the same as the Good of Plato, the "Ding-an-sich" or the transcendental Thing-in-itself of Kant, the Will of Schopenhauer, the Substantia of Spinoza, the Over-Soul of Emerson, the Unknowable of Herbert Spencer, the Divine Essence of the Heavenly Father of the Christians, and of Allah of the Mahometans. It is also the true nature of Buddha and of Christ. It pervades the universe. It is one and universal. No one can divide it; it is indivisible. This is the reality of the universe, says Vedanta.

The system of Vedanta is more critical than the Kantian system, because it shows the phenomenal nature of the Kantian ego, of his forms of intuition, and his categories of thought. It is also more sublime than the philosophy of Kant, because it recognises and proves the identity of the objective reality of the universe with-the subjective reality of the ego. Kant did not realize that the Thing-in-itself ("Ding-an-sich") of the objective world and the "Ding-an-sich") of the subjective world are one. In no other system of philosophy has this oneness been so clearly explained and so strongly emphasized as it is in Vedanta. Professor Max Muller says: "This constitutes the unique character of Vedanta, unique compared with every other philosophy of the world which has not been influenced by it, directly or indirectly". There have been many European philosophies which have denied the existence of the external world, but not one of them has ventured to deny the apparent reality of the ego, of the senses, of the mind, and of their inherent forms. In this respect Vedanta holds a most unique position among the philosophies of the world. After lifting the Self or the true nature of the ego, Vedanta unites it with the essence of Divinity, which is absolutely pure, perfect, immortal, unchangeable, and' one. No philosopher, not even Plato, Spinoza, Kant, Hegel, or Schopenhauer, has reached that height of philosophic thought. Professor Max Muller declares: "None of our philosophers, not excepting Heraclitus, Plato, Kant, or Hegel, has ventured to erect such a spire, never frightened by storms or lightnings. Stone follows on stone, in regular succession after once the first step has been made, after once it has been clearly seen that in the beginning there can have been but One, as there will be but One in the end, whether we call it Atman or Brahman."

Although Vedanta has united heaven and earth, God and man, Brahman and Atman, still it has destroyed nothing in the phenomenal world. It accepts all the ultimate conclusions of modern science; but at the same time it says that Truth is one and not many, yet there can be many expressions and various manifestations of the one Truth. Furthermore, it maintains that the aim of the higher philosophy is not merely to ascertain the established conjunctions of events which constitute the order of the universe, or to record the phenomena which it exhibits to our observation and refer them to the general laws, but also to lead the human mind from the realm of the knowable to that which is beyond the knowable. We are now living in the realm of the knowable; but that which teaches simply the laws which govern the knowable phenomena is not the highest kind of philosophy. We must know the laws of the knowable, yet at the same time we should aspire to go beyond the knowable and plunge into the realm of the Infinite. If any philosophy can help us in this attempt, then it must be higher than the ordinary system which keeps us within the limits of the knowable. Vedanta philosophy guides us above all knowable objects of perception, and directs our souls toward the Eternal Absolute Being, wherein we find the solution of all problems and the answer to all questions. Its attempt is to trace the relation between the soul and God, not by any unscientific method, but by the most rigorous processes of logic and reason, starting from the ultimate generalisations of the various branches of science.

True philosophy must construct a theory which will be the simplest in its nature, and yet at the same time will explain all the vital problems which the science of the phenomenal-knowable can never explain, and which will harmonize with the highest form of universal religion, without destroying the loftiest aspirations of the human soul. True philosophy in the widest sense must perform three great functions. First, it must coordinate the ultimate results 'arrived at by special branches of knowledge which we call sciences, and, taking up those conclusions, it must form the widest generalisations possible. When it does this, it is called phenomenology. Herbert Spencer's philosophy performs this function most wonderfully, but it leaves out the vital problems which perplex the minds of the greatest philosophers as unsolvable mysteries. Herbert Spencer does not explain all these problems, but without finding their true solution our lives will not be worth living. We must find an explanation, we must solve all the problems which disturb the peace of our souls; and if any system will help us, we will study it, follow its teachings, and satisfy our questioning minds. Secondly, true philosophy must investigate the realm of knowledge and trace its source. You know that you are sitting here and listening: where does this 'knowledge come from? The minds of even the greatest thinkers have become confused in trying to answer this question. A philosophy which does this is called Epistomology. The philosophy of Kant, Hegel, Fichte, and others has performed this function. In his "Elements of General Philosophy" George Croom Robertson says: "Epistomology is just philosophy, because it deals with things, deals with being; it deals with things going beyond bare experience, but it treats of them in relation to the fact of knowing. Thus an epistomologist cannot help being an ontologist, because his theory of knowledge must treat about things also as being. He must also be a metaphysician, because he is concerned with the whole range of things beyond the physical; he must be a philosopher in being other and more than a man of science, or concerned with things in a way in which science is not "Science" with its various branches, directs us up to a certain point, and cannot go further; but where science ends, there is the beginning of true philosophy. The third function which true philosophy performs is that of leading our minds into the realm of the Absolute, of the Unknown, and then it solves the problems of life and death. It explains the origin of the universe and of individual existence, and the purpose of evolution. On the plane of relativity the perfect solution of these vital problems can never be found. Furthermore, when this phase of true philosophy directs our minds toward the Infinite, it helps us in becoming free from all limitations of ignorance and selfishness. These limitations are the greatest bondage that we are now suffering from, and, by performing this function, true philosophy lays the foundation of the highest form of monistic religion. No philosophy in the world performs these three functions so satisfactorily as Vedanta. Hence we may say that Vedanta is the most complete of all systems.

Philosophy and religion must always be in perfect harmony. Ernest Haeckel, in his "Riddle of the Universe tries to give a foundation to monistic religion; but his monism is one sided, because he says that the ultimate substance of the universe is unintelligent. His insentient substance may be compared with Kapila's Prakriti, which is eternal and unintelligent". According to Vedanta, however, the final substance of the universe is Brahman, which is Sat or absolute existence, Chit or absolute intelligence, and Ananda or absolute bliss. Vedanta teaches that that which is the substance of our souls must possess intelligence, consciousness, and bliss fulness. Thus Vedanta lays the true foundation of a universal religion which is monistic or non dualistic. The monistic religion of Vedanta does not admit the Sankhyan theory of the plurality of Purushas, or individual souls, which are eternal and infinite by nature, but on the contrary, by following the strict rules of logic, it establishes that the Infinite must be .one and not many. From one many have come into existence, and the individual souls are but so many images or reflections of the Absolute Brahman. It teaches that the true nature of the soul is Divine. From the Absolute Brahman the phenomenal universe rises, and in the end returns into the Brahman. The religion of Vedanta admits the existence of Iswara, the personal God, who is the first born Lord of the universe, who starts the evolution of Prakriti, who loves all living creatures and can be loved and worshipped in return. In Vedanta the Prakriti of the Sankhya philosophy is called Maya, which is the divine energy of the Absolute Brahman. Maya does not mean illusion, as some scholars think; but it is that power which produces time, space, and causation, as also the phenomenal appearances which exist on the relative plane. Thus we see that the system of Vedanta is both philosophy and religion. Of the tree of knowledge, philosophy is the flower and religion is the fruit, so they must go together. Religion is nothing but the practical side of philsophy, and philosophy is the theoretical side of religion.

In India a true philosopher is not a mere speculator but a spiritual man. He does not believe in certain theories which cannot be carried into practice in everyday life; what he believes he lives, and therefore practical philosophy is still to be found in India. For example, an Indian philosopher who follows Kanada, and believes in the existence of a personal God as the essence of his soul, does not merely accept this theoretically, but he tries to realise it in his daily life. A Buddhist, again, will explain all the most abstruse problems, and at the same time you will see that he is living out his beliefs. So with a follower of the Sankhya system, or of Vedanta: they are not mere speculative philosophers, but they live spiritual lives and strive to attain God-consciousness. In India, if any one writes voluminous works and leads a worldly life, he is not considered a true philosopher; but in the West a man can become a philosopher by simply sitting in his library and writing a book, although his every day life may be far from spiritual.

A friend of mine, being asked whether India had produced a philosopher like Ralph Waldo Emerson, replied: "America has produced one Emerson, but in India you will find an Emerson every five miles." This is not a great exaggeration, and the reason, as I have already said, is that the Hindus not only theorise but live philosophy, Hindu minds are extremely logical. They will not accept any theory which does not harmonise with logic and reason. Therefore you will scarcely find an irrational doctrine or dogma in the religion of Vedanta. Freedom of thought, as I have already said, has always prevailed in India since the Vedic period. For this reason Christian missionaries meet with the greatest opposition when they preach to the Hindus the unscientific and illogical doctrines and dogmas of their faith. When, for instance, they try to teach them the creation of the universe in six days as given in Genesis, the Hindus smile at the missionaries and reject their statements as unscientific and irrational. Similarly they will not listen to other Christian dogmas, like infant damnation, eternal perdition of the heathen, etc.

The philosophy and religion of Vedanta embrace all the sciences and philosophies of the world, accepting their latest conclusions, and classify them according to their order of merit. Consequently the universality of Vedanta is unique and unparalleled. In this system the people of India find the ultimate truths of all science of all philosophies, as well as of all religions. It is so popular because it solves the problems concerning the origin and final aim of earthly life, fulfils the highest aspiration of human souls, and inculcates that the true nature of the soul is immortal by its birthright. Vedanta maintains that, if the soul were mortal by nature, it could never become immortal, for that which could be made immortal could be unmade. This is an argument which cannot be refuted, and it has taken such hold of the logical mind of the Hindus that, even when they are converted to other faiths, they cannot believe that the soul, which is by nature a child of God, can ever be made immortal by Christ.

Vedanta has the largest following, and is the prevailing philosophy of India today. Since the eighth century A.D., when, after the decline of Buddhism, it was revived by the earnest efforts of its commentator, Sri Sankaracharya, who is now regarded as the greatest philosopher of the world, the Vedanta philosophy has taken firm root in the remotest corner of every Hindu community, from the highest to the lowest, and has overshadowed all other systems of philosophic thought, Professor Max Muller, in the preface to his "Six Systems of Philosophy' writes: "Other philosophies do exist and have some following, but Vedanta has the largest"; and he also affirms that Vedanta is both a philosophy and a religion by saying: "For all practical purposes, the Vedantist would hold that the whole phenomenal world, both in its subjective and objective character, should be accepted as real. It is as real as anything can be to the ordinary mind; it is not mere emptiness, as the Buddhists maintain. And thus the Vedanta philosophy leaves to every man a wide sphere of real usefulness, and places him under a law as strict and binding as anything can be in this transitory life; it leaves him a Deity to worship as omnipotent and majestic as the deities of any other religion. It has room for almost every religion; nay, it embraces them all.

...The dawn of Aryan civilisation broke for the first time on the horizon, not of Greece or Rome, not of Arabia or Persia, but of India, which may be called the motherland of metaphysics, philosophy, logic, astronomy, science, art, music, and medicine, as well as of truly ethical religion. Although students in the schools and colleges of modern Europe and America are generally taught that the Greeks and Romans were the fathers of European civilisation and that philosophy and science first arose in ancient Greece, still it has been proved by the Oriental scholars of Europe and by all impartial students of history that ancient Greece was greatly indebted to India for many of her best ideas in philosophy, science and intellectual culture, as also for many of her ethical and spiritual ideals.

If we read the writing and historical accounts left by Pliny, Strabo, Megasthenes, Herodotus, Porphyry and a host of other ancient authors of different countries, we shall see how highly the civilisation of India was regarded by them. In fact, between the years 1500 and 500 B.C., the Hindus were so far advanced in religion, metaphysics, philosophy, science, art, music and medicine that no other nation could stand as their rival, or compete with them in any of these branches of knowledge. On the contrary, many of the nations which came in contact with the Hindus through trade or otherwise, accepted the Hindu ideas and moulded their own after the Hindu pattern. For instance, the science of geometry, as I have already said, was first invented in India by the Hindus from the Vedic rules for the construction of sacrificial altars; from these rules they gradually developed geometry and it has been admitted by the great scholars that the world owes its first lesson in this science, not to Greece, but to India. The geometrical theorem that the square of the hypotenuse of a rectangular triangle is equal to the squares of its sides was ascribed by the Greeks to Pythagoras, but it was known in India at least two centuries before Pythagoras was born. It was contained in the two rules: "(1) The square of the diagonal of a square is twice as large as that square; and (2) The square of the diagonal of an oblong is equal to the square of both its sides". These rules formed a part of the Sulva Sutras, which date from the eighth century before Christ. There is a Greek tradition that Pythagoras visited India, and most probably he did, because in his writings we find such ideas as were very common among the Hindus, but which were unknown to other nations. Probably he learned from the Hindus his first lessons in geometry, mathematics, the doctrine of preexistence and transmigration of souls and of final beatitude, ascetic observances, prohibition of eating flesh, vegetarianism, the conception of the virtue of numbers and lastly, the idea of a fifth element, which was unknown in Greece and Egypt at that ancient time. The Egyptians and Greeks admitted four elements, but ether as an element was known only among the Hindus of those days. All these things were taught by the Hindus centuries before the time of Pythagoras. Prof. E.W. Hopkins admits this in his "Religions of India", as you will recall from the first lecture, when he says: "Before the Sixth Century B.C. all the religious philosophical ideas of Pythagoras are current in India".

Geometry gradually fell out of use among the Hindus and geometrical truths were represented by algebra and arithmetic. The Greeks could not rival the Hindus in the science of numbers. The world indeed owes decimal notation of India. The Arabs first learned it from the Hindus and then introduced it into Europe. It was unknown to the Greeks and Romans, and arithmetic as a practical science would have been impossible without decimal notation. The Hindus have also given algebra (Vijaganita) to the Western world through the Arabs, who translated it in the eighth century A.D.; and Leonardo da Pisa first introduced it into Europe in the thirteenth century. So the world received its first lesson in algebra from India. The Hindus were also the first teachers of plane and spherical trigonometry. The great Indian mathematician, Bhaskaracharya, who lived from 1114-1150 A.D., wrote exhaustive treatises on all these subjects, and his works contain solutions of remarkable problems which were not achieved in Europe until the seventeenth and eighteenth centuries. In astronomical observations, the Hindus were the first to fix the lunar mansions, lunar zodiac, and the divisions of the constellations. The Chinese and Arabs borrowed these from, India. The Hindus first developed the science of music from the chanting of the Vedic hymns. The Sama Veda was especially meant for music. And the scale with seven notes and three octaves was known in India centuries before the Greeks had it. Probably the Greeks learned it from the Hindus. It will be interesting to you to know that Wagner was indebted to the Hindu science of music, especially for his principal idea of the "leading motive", and this is perhaps the reason why it is so difficult for many Western people to understand Wagner's music. He became familiar with Eastern music through Latin translations, and his conversation on this subject with Schopenhauer is probably already familiar to you.

The Western world, again, owes its first lesson in medicine to India. In the preceding lecture I gave proofs that Alexander not only had in his camp Hindu physicians, but that he preferred them to Greek physicians. Megasthenes, Nearchus and Arrian spoke highly of the wonderful healing powers of the Hindu physicians. In 1837 Dr. Royle, of King's College, London, wrote his celebrated essay on "Hindu Medicine", in which he showed that Hippocrates, the father of medicine, who lived in Greece in the fourth century B.C., borrowed his *Materia Medica* from India. Dr. Royle says, "We owe our first system of medicine to the Hindus".

Herodotus, who lived in the fifth century B.C, states that the Hindus were the greatest nation of that age. He also writes that the Hindus had trade with Egypt, while from other sources we gather that they had trade with Babylon and Syria. From another authentic source we learn that there was a Hindu philosopher who visited Socrates at Athens, a fact which Prof. Max Muller confirms in his book on "Psychological Religion". This Hindu philosopher, we are told, had a conversation with the great Greek philosopher. He asked in what the philosophy of Socrates consisted, and Socrates replied that his philosophy consisted in inquiries about the life of man, upon which the Hindu philosopher smiled and answered. "How can you know things human without first knowing things divine?" And that is an answer which could not have been given by any other than a Hindu, because the Hindus ascribed all true knowledge to Divine origin, and did not care much for the knowledge of anything human before knowing God.

Ralph Waldo Emerson says: "Plato was a synthesis of Europe and Asia and a decidedly Oriental element pervades his philosophy, giving it a sunrise color". In fact, in teaching asceticism, Plato was more of a Hindu than a Greek, because, of all nations, the Greeks were least ascetic. My friend, Professor Edward Howard Griggs, in his lecture on the "Philosophy of Plato" before the Vedanta Society of New York, also admitted this in saying: "Plato's belief in the conquest of the senses, as the only means of attaining true knowledge, was preeminently Oriental and non-Greek". Moreover, if we study Plato carefully, comparing his ideas with those of the Upanishads and other Vedic writings, we find that his well known figure of the man chained in the cave is merely an allegorical presentation of the Vedanta doctrine of Maya, that the phenomenal world is like a dream; while his other figure of the chariot was a favorite theme of the Vedic writers who lived centuries before Plato. In the Katha Upanishad, for instance, we read: "This body may be compared to a chariot, intellect to the charioteer, mind to the reins, the five senses to the horses, whose path is the object of senses". Sir William Jones, the first eminent Sanskrit scholar among the English, confirming this fact, writes that "it is impossible to read the Vedanta, or the many fine compositions in illustration of it, without believing that Pythagoras and Plato derived their sublime theories from the same fountain with the Indian sages".

Professor Max Muller and other oriental scholars maintain, as you know, that the logic of Aristotle was perhaps a Greek presentation of the Hindu logic. You will also remember that Professor Hopkins writes, in his "Religions of India", that Thales and Parmenides were both anticipated by the sages of India, while the Eleatic School appears merely a reflection of the Upanishads. He even suggests that the doctrines propounded by Anaximander and Heraclitus might not have been known first in Greece. We should, indeed, bear in mind that after the invasion of India by Alexander the Great the connection between India and Greece became closer than ever before, and many Hindu philosophers lived at Athens and in other parts of Greece. They were known as Gymnosophists, or Hindu philosophers from India. At that time Alexandria became the center of trade and commerce between India and Greece, and there was great opportunity for interchange of ideas between the Hindu and Western nations. Porphyry speaks of the wise men from India in high terms of praise for their wisdom, morality and knowledge of the mysteries of the universe. In regard to Neo-Platonism, Professor Garbe has said that Plotinus was in perfect agreement with the Hindu philosophers and that his disciple Porphyry knew of the Yoga doctrine of union with the Deity. It was unknown to any of the Western nations, like the Hebrews, Parsees, or Egyptians. Through Plato and his followers, the Neo-Platonists, Stoics and Philo of Alexandria were also influenced by the Hindu Philosophy. The idea of the Logos which formed the cornerstone of the philosophy of Plato, of the Neo-Platonists, of Philo, and later of the Fourth Gospel, first arose in India. In the Vedas we find reference to it and it has moulded Hindu thought, as well as the religious ideals of other nations.

Christianity as a religion owes a great deal to India. This may startle some of our friends, but from the historical standpoint it is true. If we read the religious history of the East, we find many evidences which are undeniable. For instance, Asoka, who lived in 260 B.C., had his edicts inscribed on pillars of stone during his lifetime and in one of those edicts we read that he sent Buddhist missionaries to different parts of the world, from Siberia to Ceylon, from China to Egypt, and that, for two centuries before the advent of Jesus, the Buddhist missionaries preached the sublime ethics of Buddha in Syria, Palestine and Alexandria. The same ethical ideas were afterwards repeated and emphasised by Christ. The Christian historian Mahafi, speaking about those Buddhist missionaries, declared it to be a fact that they were the fore runners of Christ. These preachers influenced the Jewish sect known as the Essenes; and the Roman historian Pliny, who lived between 23 and 79 A.D., described the mode of living of the Essenes that they lived like hermits, without having any possessions or any sex relation, being celibates and associates of palm trees. It can be shown that they belonged to the sect founded by the Buddhist monks from India, who lived in Syria, Palestine, and Egypt. Philosophers like Schelling and Schopenhauer, and Christian thinkers like Dean Mansel and D. Millman, admit that the sect of the Essenes arose through the influence of the Buddhist missionaries who came from India. Moreover, it is a well known fact that John the Baptist was an Essene. Ernest Renan, speaking of John the Baptist, says: "He led there a life like that of a Yogi of India, clothed with skins or cloth of camel's hair, having for food only locusts and wild honey. We might imagine ourselves transported to the banks of the Ganges, if special features had not revealed in this recluse the last descendant of the grand prophets of Israel." Again he says: "The teachers of the young were also at times a species of anchorites, resembling to some extent the Gurus (spiritual preceptors) of Brahminism. In fact, might there not in this be a remote influence of the Mounts (sages) of India? Perhaps some of those wandering Buddhist monks who overran the world, as the first Franciscans did in later times, preaching by their actions and converting people who knew not their language, might have turned their steps towards Judea, as they certainly did towards Syria and Babylon. ... Babylon had become for some time a true focus of

Buddhism. Boudasp (Bodhisattva) was reputed a wise Chaldean, and the founder of Sabeism. Sabeism was, as its etymology indicates, baptism" And he continues; "We may believe, at all events, that many of the external practices of John, of the Essenes, and of the Jewish spiritual teachers of this time, were derived from influences then but recently received from the far East. The fundamental practice which gave to the sect of John its character, and which has given him his name, has always had its center in lower Chaldea, and, constitutes a religion which is practised there to this day. This practice was baptism or total immersion. Ablutions were already familiar to the Jews, as they were to all the religions of the East The Essenes had given them a peculiar extension".

Thus we see that baptism by water was introduced among the Essenes by the Buddhist missionaries, having originated in India. Baptism afterwards became the principal ceremony at the time of the initiation of the disciple in the religion of John. The life of Jesus the Christ as described in the Synoptic Gospels, the immaculate conception of a virgin mother, the miraculous birth, the story of the slaughter of infants by Herod, and the chief events of his life, all these seem like repetitions of what happened in the lives of Krishna (1400 B.C.) and of Buddha (547 B.C.). In fact, the idea of the incarnation of God is purely a Hindu idea. It was not known among the Jews. The Jews never accepted Christ as the incarnation of Divinity, but from the Vedic period the Hindus accepted many Avataras or Incarnations of the Lord in a human form, and this is at the foundation of the religion of the Hindus. Many of the famous parables of Jesus the Christ existed among the Hindus and Buddhists of the pre Christian era. In the Gospel of Buddha, for instance, we find the parables of the prodigal son and of the marriage feast, which were taught by Buddha to his disciples about five centuries B.C., and they resemble in every way the similar parables' of Jesus the Christ. The Roman Catholics have taken a great many of their ideas—their form of worship, the monastic life, the nunnery and the idea of purgatory—from the Buddhists of India. In the religious history of the world, Buddha was the first to organise communities of monks and nuns and to establish monasteries and nunneries. Under cover of the legend of Barlaam and Josaphat, the story of Buddha has found a niche in the row of canonised Catholic saints and has his Saint day in the calendar of the Greek and Roman churches.

The Buddhist missionaries and preachers also influenced the faith of the Gnostics and Manicheans, and introduced the idea of reincarnation among them. Many of the early church Fathers, like Origen, admitted that the soul existed before birth and would be born again, that this was not the first or the last time that we had come or would come to this world. The doctrine of preexistence and reincarnation of souls was accepted by the majority of the Christians until it was suppressed in 538 A.D by Justinian, who passed this law: "Whoever shall support the mythical presentation of the preexistence of the soul and the consequently wonderful opinion of its return, let him be Anathema," It was foreign to Judaism until about the eighth century A.D., when under the influence of the Hindu mystics it was adopted by the Karaites and other Jewish sects. The Jewish Encyclopedia says: "Only with the spread of the Cabala, did it begin to take root in Judaism, and then it gained believers even among men who were little inclined toward mysticism." And again: "Like Origen and other church Fathers the Cabalists used as their main argument in favor of the doctrine of metempsychosis the justice of God!"

The Sanskrit grammar of Panini, who, according to Max Muller, was the greatest grammarian that the world has ever seen, has given a key to the science of comparative philology. Many of the English words which we commonly use can be traced back to a Sanskrit origin. For instance: Mother, in Latin mater, is in Sanskrit Mater; father, in Latin pater, is in Sanskrit Pitar; brother, in Sanskrit Bhratar; sister, Swasar; daughter, Duhitar; path, in Sanskrit Patha serpent, Sarpa; bond, Bandha; etc. The word "punch" has an interesting history. It originally meant "five" in Sanskrit; so the expression, "Give him a punch," means literally "Give him five fingers." We also use the name "punch" for the drink, which implies that it is made up of five ingredients.

In the last lecture, I showed how the fables of Esop and Pilpay originated in India. Indeed, these stories of animals, with their wonderful Hindu morals, have influenced the young minds of Europe and America for many centuries. I think no child is brought up without studying some of them and learning the morals attached to them. Roman law and Roman jurisprudence also were perhaps not left uninfluenced by the more perfect system of ancient Hindu law.

Now, I will show you the more recent influence of India upon Western civilisation. Those who have studied Schopenhauer's philosophy have undoubtedly noticed that he was full of Buddhistic ideas, as well as of the principles of the Vedanta philosophy. He paid a great tribute to the latter by his celebrated saying, "There is no study more beneficial and elevating to mankind than the study of the Upanishads (Vedanta). It has been the solace of my life, and it will be the solace of my death." And Max Muller declares, "if philosophy is meant to be a preparation for a happy death, or Euthenasia, I know of no better preparation for it than the Vedanta philosophy", while Schopenhauer's direct disciple, Paul Deussen, writes in his, "Philosophy of the Upanishads" "God, the sole author of all good in us, is not, as in the Old Testament, a being contrasted with and distinct from us, but rather .... Our divine self. This and much more we may learn from the Upanishads: we shall learn the lesson if we are willing to put the finishing touch to the Christian consciousness, and to make it on all sides consistent and complete." In fact, the philosophy of modern Europe has obtained a new life since the introduction of the doctrines of Vedanta into it. Carlyle was influenced by the teachings of Krishna through the English version of the Bhagavad Gita, first translated by Charles Wilkins during the administration of Warren Hastings and now well known to you as the "Song Celestial". Many other translations have also been published in Europe and America. Frederick Schlegel, Victor Cousin, Amiel, Paul Deussen, Max Muller and Emerson were great advocates of the Vedanta Philosophy. Emerson was, indeed, the pioneer of Hindu thought in America. He says in his Journal that the study of the Upanishads was a favorite recreation with him. Perhaps you have read his poem on Brahman, which he calls "Brahm", it begins with this celebrated verse:

"If the red slayer thinks he slays,
or if the slain thinks he is slain.
They know not well the sublet ways
I keep, and pass, and turn again."

This is almost a literal translation of a passage in the Bhagavad Gita, which runs thus:

"He who thinketh it to be a slayer and he who thinketh it to be slain, both of these know not, for it neither kitteth nor is killed" (chap. II. Verse 19).

Like Emerson, the Concord sage, Thoreau, was also deeply imbued with the sublime teachings of Vedanta. "The Hindus", he writes, are more serenely and thoughtfully religious than the Hebrews. They have, perhaps, a purer, more independent, and impersonal knowledge of God. Their religious books describe the first inquisitive and contemplative access to God; the Hebrew Bible, a conscientious return, a grosser and more personal repentance. Repentance is not a free and fair highway to God. A wise man will dispense which repentance. It is shocking and passionate. God prefers that you approach him thoughtfully, not penitent, though you are the chief of sinners. It is only by forgetting yourself that you draw near to Him.

"The calmness and gentleness with which the Hindu philosophers approach and discourse on forbidden themes is admirable".

"What extracts from the Vedas I have read fall on me like the light of a higher and purer luminary, which describes a loftier course through a purer stratum, free from particulars, simple, universal. It rises on me like the full moon after the stars have come out, wading through some far summer stratum of sky".

"The Vedant teaches how", "by forsaking religious rites", the votary may "obtain purification of mind".

"One wise sentence is worth the State of Massachusetts many times over".

"The Vedas contain a sensible account of God".

"The religion and philosophy of the Hebrew are those of a wilder and ruder tribe, wanting the civility and intellectual refinement and subtlety of the Hindus".

"I do not prefer one religion or philosophy to another. I have no sympathy with the bigotry and ignorance which makes transient and partial and puerile distinctions between one man's faith and another's, as Christian and heathen. I pray to be delivered from narrowness, partiality, exaggeration, bigotry. To the philosopher, all sects, all nations, are alike. I like Brahma, Hari, or Buddha, the Great Spirit, as well as God."

Today the whole Western world is permeated with Hindu thoughts and ideals. The educated men and women of Europe and America, who have outgrown the superstitions, doctrines, and dogmas of orthodox Christianity, are finding the right solutions of the problems of life and death, and of the riddles of the universe, as also the greatest comfort and happiness in the universal religion of Vedanta, which is in perfect harmony with the science, logic, and philosophy of modern Europe. Today the moral influence of Buddhism and the ethics of Vedanta are strongly felt in all European and American communities. You see how many vegetarians are springing up, how many people now prefer a vegetarian diet to animal flesh. I saw the other day in New York a hospital for dogs and cats, but, as I have already told you, such a hospital was built in 260 B.C. by the Buddhist emperor, Asoka. Then, again, the interest in concentration, meditation, breathing exercises, New Thought, etc., which is to be found at present all through Europe and America, is the result of Eastern influence. Mrs. Eddy's early editions of "Science and Health had quotations from the Bhagavad Gita; and Celia Thaxter, we know, was deeply influenced by the teachings of Krishna, gathered from the same source". The Theosophists have, indeed, disseminated the Hindu teachings most widely all over the world. Even in Mexico I discovered that the teachings of Vedanta were spreading rapidly.

From very ancient times the Hindus as a nation have practised the sublime ethical precept of non resistance of evil, and the grand moral doctrine of returning good for evil and "love thy neighbor as thyself." "Love thy neighbor as thyself" was taught by Christ, but why? The reason was not given by Him. In the Vedas we find the reason: "Thou shalt love thy neighbor because thou art thy neighbor in spirit. Thou art one with him." "*Tat twam asi*" "That art Thou." Love means expression of oneness. The Hindus have always practised these higher ethical virtues, but as a result India has been invaded again and again by the greedy nations of Europe and Asia. Today they have been enslaved by the swords of a Christian nation, whose Master proclaimed before the world the doctrine of non resistance of evil, of returning good for evil, and of loving one's enemies. As nations, the so called Christian nations of Europe do not follow the path of their Master, do not practise non resistance of evil, do not love their enemies; on the contrary, they worship Mammon, and seek worldly success and material prosperity instead of the Kingdom of Heaven. They send missionaries as forerunners of conquest and pioneers for territorial possession. They do not spread peace and goodwill among the people, but fire and guns, as we have seen lately in the British expedition to Tibet. We cannot forget how the poor, innocent Tibetans were mowed down by Maxim guns. We cannot forget how the Portuguese and Dutch Christians held in one hand the Bible and in the other a gun, and demolished the Hindu temples in India. We cannot forget how the Christian missionaries, under the name of religion, destroyed the monuments of Buddhism in Japan until they were driven out by the Japanese Government in 1614 A.D. The Hindu and Buddhist missionaries, on the contrary, have always carried, instead of fire and sword, the gospel of peace and goodwill, and have civilised the nations.

Think what Buddhism has done for China and Japan, for Tibet and Burmah! The whole civilisation of Japan is indebted to Buddhism for its art, as for most other things. Buddhism was introduced into Japan in the sixth century after Christ, and since that time has lived there in absolute peace and harmony with Shintoism and Confucianism. Buddhism was introduced into China in 65 A.D., and it has existed among the Chinese for nearly two thousand years without destroying anything of Taoism and Confucianism, at the same time broadening the religious ideals of the nation, humanizing and civilising them. Lafcadio Hearn, in his book on Japan, shows how much Buddhism has done for Japan; and those who have read "The Soul of a People," by H. Fielding Hall, cannot help admiring the humane, loving, and spiritual qualities of the Buddhist people. Religious toleration has always been practised by the Hindus and Buddhists. When the Parsees were driven out of Persia by the Mohametans, they took refuge in India, where they are now flourishing and living unmolested. Under the influence of this religious toleration of the Hindus, Western nations, especially the English, are beginning to learn and practise it. The Hindus and Buddhists have never robbed their neighbours to enrich themselves, but they have given to the world the highest moral and spiritual truths, not in mere theories, but by setting their noble examples. The Hindus and Buddhists have always been the true spiritual teachers of the world; they know how to preach and how to live religion. "By a strange irony of fate, today they are called barbarous and uncivilised heathens by the aggressive pioneers of European conquest."

...Practical morality and spirituality have always been considered by the Hindus as greater than mere intellectual culture. In India, religion has been the source of philosophy, science, art, music and everything. From religion the Hindus have gained their education and culture, therefore religion is a vital thing with them. It is the primary thing, while intellectual culture is secondary. The Hindus cultivate the feelings of the heart and do not care much for external reforms. It is for this reason that their civilisation is based upon the highest moral and spiritual standards. Hindu civilisation is founded, not upon the commercial and industrial interests of the people, but upon the eternal moral and spiritual laws which govern our lives. It is not like the European civilisation of today, which inspires a nation mainly to protect its self interest at the expense of other nations, and to gain material and commercial prosperity by depriving others of their rights, by robbing the weaker nations who are kind, innocent, and humane.

According to the Hindu idea, that man is civilised who is versed in the scriptures, who is learned and wise in the various branches of knowledge, who is truthful, unselfish, and who obeys the moral laws, who helps the poor and distressed, who returns good for evil, and who conquers hatred by love, avarice by generosity. These are the high moral virtues which should adorn the character of a thoroughly civilised man. A civilised man must always cultivate these virtues, and control the brute impulses and animal propensities with which he is born. By these virtues the civilised man is distinguished from a barbarous savage, as also from lower animals. A civilised man or woman must have polished manners, not simply as an external form, as we see in Europe today, but they must proceed from the feelings of the heart. European civilisation, on the contrary, has left moral and spiritual standards in the background and made material prosperity and intellectual culture the chief factors of civilisation. The old brutal law of "might is right" is still in its ascendancy in the civilisation of the West. The West looks mainly to externals, but India looks chiefly to the internal. With the former, worldly prosperity is the goal, and intellectual preeminence is its watchword. With the latter, the attainment of spiritual perfection is the highest aim of civilisation and the cultivation of moral virtues is a necessary steps or auxiliary. In Europe, religion has always retarded the progress of true civilisation and freedom of thought by the inquisition, and by continuous persecution on the part of priests and clergy. Think of the fate of Galileo, Gairdino Bruno, and a host of other eminent thinkers of the Middle Ages! Consequently religion has been put aside from practical daily life. But freedom of thought must be the constant companion of true civilisation. Social and political freedom are also the outcome of the most advanced kind of civilisation. Freedom is the goal for every man, but that freedom must be based upon moral and spiritual laws.

...Long before the civil laws of the Romans, which gave the foundation for the legislation of Europe and of America, were codified by justinian, the Hindu laws of Manu were closely observed and strictly followed by the members of Hindu society in general. Many of the Oriental scholars, having compared the digest of Justinian and the Mosaic laws of the Old Testament with the Hindu laws, have arrived at the conclusion that the code of Manu was related to them as a father is to his child. Yet the Hindu law-givers only repeated and codified the ethical principles which were inculcated in the Vedas. Following the teachings of the Vedas, the Hindu legislator gave equal rights to men and women by saying: "Before the creation of this phenomenal universe, the first born Lord of all creatures divided his own self into two halves, so that one half should be male and the other half female". This illustration has established in the minds of the Hindus the fundamental equality of man and woman. Just as the equal halves of a fruit possess the same nature, the same attributes, and the same properties in equal proportion, so man and woman, being the equal halves of the same substance, possess equal rights, equal privileges, and equal powers. This idea of the equality of man and woman was the corner stone of that huge structure of religion and ethics among the Hindus which has stood for so many ages the ravages of time and change, defying the onslaughts of the short sighted critics of the world. Therefore, in India, whatever is claimed for the man may also be claimed for the woman, there should be no partiality shown for either man or woman, according to the ethical, moral, and religious standards of the Hindus.

3

Collection from the Complete Works of Sister Nivedita

...I remember that some of the greatest men and women that ever lived have been born in India. I remember that from India emanated the only religion that ever put the missionary question on a true educational basis; I remember that amongst military leaders two thousand years ago India produced her Napoleon Bonaparte, in Chandragupta, the Shudra who unified a continent; that amongst statesmen she bore Ashoka and Akbar; that in science we owe mathematics and astronomy and geometry to her; that in philosophy and in Literature she has achieved the highest rank.

I remember too that this greatness is not dead in the country. No longer ago than 1750 Raja Jai Singh concluded that European astronomical tables contained an error which he was able to correct. Subsequent science, it is said, stood by the Indian astronomer. Within the century that is leaving us Ram Chandra has solved, by intuitive methods, problems of maxima and minima hitherto unfinished, and India has given proof that she can yet add to her scientific laurels.

Seeing all this, I read a message of great hope for humanity, what may be the truth about the military careers of nations, I do not know. It may be that in rude activities there are periods of growth and flourishing and decay. But if a people fix their hope upon their own humanisation, it is not so. The curve of civilisation is infinite and spiral. The dominion of the human mind and spirit has yet to be exhausted.

But still-where-why-is this humanizing process the essential life of India, more than of other countries? What differentiates the Indian training from others? I find one answer which outweighs all others in my estimate. It is this. The special greatness of Indian life and character depends more than on any other feature, on the place that is given to Woman in the social scheme. What? You will say, what about child marriage and child widowhood, and the grievances of woman? I am not going to speak of woman as the wife. There must be unhappy marriages in India as elsewhere, though I have seen none but the happy, and they have seemed to me to represent a tie more tender and intimate than I have often witnessed. But wifehood in India is not woman's central function. That is motherhood. As mother, an Indian woman is supreme. The honour that a man does here by the simple words "my wife," he does better there by saying "the mother of my children." Sons worship their mothers as the ideal. Motherhood is the ideal relation to the world. Let us free ourselves from selfseeking as the mother does. Let us be incapable of jealousy as is a mother to her child. Let us give to the uttermost. Let us love most those who need most. Let us be undiscriminating in our service. Such is the Indian woman's conception of a perfect life. Such is the moral culture with which she surrounds her children. Can you ask what is its effect? I sat one day hour after hour beside a body of twelve who was dying of plague. The home was of the poorest, a mud hut with a thatched roof. The difficulty lay in keeping the patient isolated from his family. There was one woman who came and went about the bedside perpetually, in an utter recklessness of her own safety, and at last I ventured to remonstrate, pointing out that my presence was of no use, if I could not save her this exposure. She obeyed me instantly, without a word, but as she went, hid her face in her veil crying softly. It was the lad's mother. Of course I found a place where she could sit with his head on her feet, curled up behind him in comparative security, fanning him, and then, through all the hours of that hot day, till sunset came, I had a picture before me of perfect love. "Mataji! Mataji! Adored Mother!" was the name he called her by. Now and then, mistaking me for her, he smiled his perfect contentment into my eyes, and once he snatched at my hand and carried his own to his lips. And this was a child of the Calcutta slums!

But it is not the child only. The word mother is the endless shore on which all Indian souls find harbour. In moments of great agony it is not with them, "My God!" but "Oh Mother!"

A woman in the neighbourhood was wailing loudly in the dark, and the sound disturbed one who was lying ill. An attendant on the sick came down into the woman's hut to find her, and, guided by her cries, came up to her quietly and put an arm about her. The wailing ceased as suddenly as it had begun, and she fell back with long sobs; "You are my mother!" was all that she could say.

If the word "God" meant as much to us as "Mother" to this bereaved soul, what might we not reach? And to many in India it is so. The two ideas are one. Life with all its inexplicable torture and its passing gleams of joy is but the play of the Divine Motherhood of the Universe, with Her children. If we can understand this, all happenings will become alike fortunate. We must cease to discriminate. And so in every temple dedicated to this idea, the visitor enters with the prayer:

Thou, - the Giver of all blessings,
Thou, - the Giver of all desires,
Thou, - the Giver of all good,
To *Thee* our salutation.
Thee we salute, Thee we salute, Thee we salute.
Thou terrible dark Night!
Thou, the Night of delusion!
Thou, the Night of Death!
To *Thee* our salutation,
Thee we salute, Thee we salute, Thee we salute.

And this rises up daily from end to end of the country together with that other prayer to the Soul of the Universe which to me seems the most beautiful in any language.

From the unreal lead us to the Real,
From darkness lead us unto Light,
From death lead us to Immortality,
Reach us through and through ourselves
And ever more protect us – O Thou Terrible!
From ignorance, by Thy sweet compassionate face.

...I love India as the birth place of the highest and best of all religions; as the country that has the grandest mountains, the Himalayas; as the place where the sublimest of mountains are located. The country where the homes are simple; where domestic happiness is most to be found; where the woman unselfishly, unobtrusively, ungrudgingly, serves the dear ones from early morn to dewy eve; where the mother and the grandmother studies, foresees and contributes to the comfort of her belongings, regardless of her own happiness, and in the unselfishness raises womanhood to its highest eminence.

You, my sisters, each of whom I dearly love for being the daughter of this lovely land of India, each of you I urge to study the grand literatures of your East in preference to the literatures of the West. Your literature will uplift you. Cling to it. Cling to the simplicity and sobriety of your domestic lives. Keep its purity as it was in the ancient times and as it is still existing in your simple homes.

Do not let modern fashions and extravagances of the West and its modern English education spoil your reverential humility, your lovable domestic ties consisting in the loving forethought the elders display for the beloved ones, depending on them, and the resulting respectful deference filially and dutifully accorded by the young to the aged. I make this appeal not to my Hindu sisters only but also to Mohammedan and other sisters of mine too. All are my sisters being the daughters of my land of adoption and where I hope to continue the work of my revered Guru Vivekananda.

...Hinduism recognises only one proof, and that is direct perception. Even the sacred writings give as their sanction the direct perception of saints and sages, and the Vedas themselves declare that man must reach beyond the Vedas. That is to say, the books allege as their authority that realisation out of which they were written. The Jains refuse the authority of the Vedic texts. But there is less divergence between them and other sects of Hinduism than would appear on the surface. Common language and the historic acceptance of the race alike, lead up to the last great pronouncement on the subject—" By the Vedas no books are meant. They mean the accumulated treasury of spiritual laws discovered by different persons in different times."

"It is Veda," we say in India of a statement which we perceive to be profoundly true. It is held in a general way that there are two classes of Scripture, one Vedas, the other Puranas. Vedas are eternal truth. Puranas are characterised by containing stories of the creation and destruction of the world, tales of the life and death of holy persons and avatars, accounts of their miracles, and so on. These elements are commonly mixed up, but can easily be disentangled. Thus, when the Christian Gospel says, "Thou shalt love the Lord thy God with all thy heart and with all thy soul," it speaks Veda; but when is says, "Jesus was born in Bethlehem of Judea in the days of Herod the king" it is only, a Purana, and may contain some elements of error.

And so, if the word be rightly defined, it may be said that the Vedas themselves are the sanction of Buddhism, of Mohammedanism, of Christianity, and of Confucianism; but it may at the same time be claimed on behalf of India that there, and not in the West, has this fact been understood.

Some of the greatest of French and English thinkers hold that the history of the West is made into a unity by the evolution of science and its progressive application to life, from the sixth century before Christ to the present day. These thinkers maintain that Greece, Imperial Rome, and the Catholic Church have been the three integral formative influences of what we call the European mind. To the student of the Oriental history, it appears equally clear, that the history of Asia is that of a single living organism of which India may be taken as the heart and focus. Regarded thus, in relation to its surroundings, the culture to which we give the name of Indian thought becomes likewise a unity, as clear, as continuous, as consistent in its development as is the evolution of the scientific idea in the West. Considered as an appendage of Europe, India is meaningless. Taken in and for herself, and for that to which she rightly belongs, it need not surprise us if we find her the essential factor of human advance in the future as in the past.

India is the heart of Asia. Hinduism is a convenient name for the nexus of the Indian thought. It would appear that it takes some thousand to 15 hundred years to work out a single rhythm of its great pulsation. For this is about the period that divides the war of the Mahabharata from Buddha, Buddha from Shankaracharya, and Shankaracharya from Ramakrishna, in whom the immense pile reaches the crowning selfconsciousness. Of the long prehistoric evolution 'that went to the building up of the Mahabharata, Great India, the heroic age, we can say little, for nothing is left to us, save the legend of Sita and Rama, out of the night of time. Yet we know that this period must have been long. To allow, a period of three thousand years seems not too much. Behind this again loom the millenia spent on the tableland of Central Asia, that watershed of the world civilisation where the Aryan man entered the patriarchate, and closed the account of his first combat with Nature, having tamed the beasts, learned the use of the tools, domesticated corn and fire, produced the fruit trees, and divided the week. Of the sublime dreams, the poetry and the song with which he consoled himself during those ages of Herculean struggle, the fragment known as the "Rig- Veda" still remains. And we learn therein how broad his outlook upon Nature was, even as that of the mind that declared "and the evening and the morning were the first day." How long did it last? Was it ten thousand years? Were there another five thousand years before the war of Mahabharata? However this be, the enthusiasm of the succeeding periods strikes us as extra ordinary.

There is no question that the characteristic product of the civilisation that succeeded the Great War was the forest universities, notes of whose sessions have become the Sutras and Upanishads. But we must not forget also that during the same period the Vedas were written down, and the searching scrutiny of society initiated which was later to result in those accumulations of reverent and sympathetic interpretations now known to us as the Laws of Manu.

It is only with difficulty that we realise the sense of vastness to which the thinkers of this period strove to give expression. The Celt, it has been said, strives ever towards the infinite of emotion. The Hindu, in the same way, cannot rest content, short of the infinite of thought. We see this, even so early as the hymns of the Rig Veda. "When darkness was hidden in darkness, undistinguished, like one mass of water," opens the great Anthem of Creation. Still larger is the sweep of the Upanishads— "they that see the Real in the midst of this Unreal, they that behold life in the midst of this death, they that know the One in all the changing mani foldness of this universe, unto them belongs eternal peace—unto none else, unto none else." The Vedas were the capital with which Aryan culture began its occupation of India, and these immense and subtle generalisations of the Upanishads represent the first achievement of the national mind in its new place. Surely this is the secret of the striking fact in Indian history that all great eras of rejuvenescence, like Shankaracharya's, and even minor movements of reconstruction like Guru Nanak's and Ramanuja's have had to go back to the Upanishads and place themselves in structural continuity with them. In this light we begin to suspect that the war of the Mahabharata itself represents the apparent exhaustion of Vedic inspiration at the end of the first period, and the restoration of pristine vigour by force of Krishna's personality.

The dim twilight of Indian forests in the pre-Buddhistic age is resonant, to the historic ear, with chants and prayers. But the succeeding epoch leads us into the busy life of villages and cities. For the ballads and songs of the people are crystallising now into the great Epics. Their religious activity—stirred by the sublime spectacle of a life that represents the whole of the Upanishadic culture, the national dream in its completeness which occupies itself with gathering together, and weaving into a whole, all the religious ideas innate amongst the masses, and those peculiar to the Indian environment. There is a sudden accession of force given to such practices as pilgrimage and relic worship, and Brahmin intelligence is more or less, unconsciously, preoccupied with the interpretation of images, symbols and rituals in relation to those truths which had been the first realisation of the race. The distinction and larger scope of this Buddhist period lay, to a great extent, in its political, commercial, and sub religious elements, in letters, arts, and sciences.

Certain evils must have come in the train of the ideas then elaborated, essential as they were to prove themselves in the long run to the complete fabric of Hinduism. We can understand that monastic notions may have attracted too much of the national energy out of the safe paths of the domestic virtue with a tendency to bring about not only the depletion of family life, but the disintegration of morality itself. No doubt, it was at this time, and to meet this error, that the song of the ideal sang itself so clearly, first through the lips of Kalidas, in his "Birth of the War-Lord," and again, in the final recension of the Ramayana, as the love of Sita for Rama, that glorified wifehood, before which the renunciation and faith of the cloister grow pale.

From the point of view of the purity of doctrine, we can believe, that the very breadth of the welcome extended to the religious ideas of all kinds, especially in the closing centuries of this age, had led to the undue emphasis on popular notions, to the inclusion of an unnecessary multiplicity of the symbols, and possibly to the interpretation of the symbols already existing in rude or gross ways.

But agitation against the abuses has never been the method of Hinduism. Rather, the faith has progressed by lifting repeatedly in moments of crisis, the banner of the highest ideal Already, in the era we are considering, this organic law of the national genius, the law of the Avatars, was well known. "Whenever the Dharma decays, and when that which is not Dharma prevails," then I manifest myself, For the protection of the good, for the destruction of the evil, for the firm establishment of the national righteousness, "I am born again and again." So says the Bhagavad Gita—and never was any prophecy more conclusively vindicated than this, by the appearance of Shankaracharya, early in the ninth century after Christ.

This wonderful boy—for he died at the age of thirty two — was born at the end of the eighth century, and had already completed a great mission when most men are still dreaming of the future. The characteristic product of Oriental culture is always a commentary. By this form of literature the future is knit firmly to the past, and though the dynamic power of the connecting idea may be obscure to the foreigner, it is clearly and accurately conveyed to the Eastern mind itself. The whole of Confucianism is contained in a commentary on the Eking, or Book of Change, and European Protestantism, might almost be described as a special kind of commentary on the Christian sacred literature. The Sanskrit Sutras lend themselves to critical writing, and even demand it, in a special degree: for the word Sutra means thread, and is applied to works which are only the main, line of a given argument, and require expansion at the end of every sentence. This literary convention obtains in, all oriental countries, and must date from the period when the main function of writing was to assist memorising. Obviously, by writing a new commentary on a given Sutra, the man of genius has it in his power to readjust the relationship between a given question and the whole of current opinion. Hence it is not surprising to find that the masterpiece of Shankaracharya's life was a commentary on the Vedanta-Sutra.

The problems which faced the Indian mind during his lifetime, with the single exception that the country was then rich and prosperous, must have been curiously like those of the present day, and it is difficult to avoid the conclusion that in his eyes they assumed national dimensions. Religious practices had lost their primitive simplicity, and also perhaps their compelling power. Ideas as to national and unnational (for the word "orthodox" was but the Asiatic word for "national") were conflicting and confused. Men lived much in the thought of the recent sectarian developments of the faith, and tended to lose sight of its austere imperative, pointing to the highest realisation, of its antiquity, and its close-knit continuity. Lakshmi, Goddess of Fortune, was one of the chief objects of worship. Sects and kingdoms alike had lost their sense of mutual solidarity. Never perhaps was an Asiatic people nearer precipitating itself on a purely secular development.

At this moment the whole of the national genius awoke once more in Shankaracharya. Amidst all the brilliance and luxury of the age, in spite of the rich and florid taste of the Puranic period, his soul caught the mystic whisper of the ancient rhythm of the Vedic chants, and the dynamic power of the faith to lead the soul to superconsciousness, became for him the secret of every phase of Hinduism. He was on fire with the love of the Vedas. His own poems have something of their classical beauty and vigour, and his books may almost be described as chains of quotations from the most piercing and comprehensive sentences of the Upanishads, to which he has contributed links and rivets. Shankaracharya wandered, during his short life, from his birthplace in the South as far as the Himalayas, and everything that he came across in his travels related itself to the one focus and centre, in his mind. He accepted each worship, even that to which he was at first averse, but always because he found that the great mood of One without a second was not only the Vedic, but also the Puranic goal. This is the doctrine that he expresses in his twelve epoch making commentaries, especially in his crowning work, the commentary on the Vedanta Sutra. And this idea, known as the Adwaita Philosophy, constitutes, for the rest of the Hindu period, the actual unity of India.

Western people can hardly imagine a personality such as that of Shankaracharya. In the course of so few years to have nominated the founders of no less than ten great religious orders, of which four have fully retained their prestige to the present day; to have acquired such a mass of Sanskrit learning as to create a distinct philosophy, and impress himself on the scholarly imagination of India in a preeminence that twelve hundred years have not sufficed to shake; to have written poems whose grandeur makes them unmistakable, even to the foreign and unlearned ear; and at the same time to have lived with his disciples in all the radiant joy and simple pathos of the saints—this is greatness that we may appreciate, but cannot understand. We contemplate with wonder and delight the devotion of Francis of Assisi, the intellect of Abelard, the force and freedom of Martin Luther, and the political efficiency of Ignatius Loyola; but who could imagine all these united in one person?

Subsequent critics have painted Shankaracharya as the persecutor of Buddhists. In as much as he asserted a coordination of mythologies and doctrines instead of preaching a single exclusive method of salvation; in as much as to him, the goal was a positive, and not a negative affirmation, and in so far also as he insisted upon the worthlessness, of, ritual, apart from philosophy, of worship without illumination he may be taken as the enemy of one school or another. It is almost unnecessary to add that this enmity was purely controversial in its character, and to Buddhists of the Northern School, a clearer historic knowledge will reveal him as the very opposite of a persecutor, as, rather, another example of the race of inspired religious teachers to which their own apostle, Nagarjuna, belonged.

Buddhism as a whole, with the succeeding Puranism, had been the creation of the lay mind, the creation of the people. The work of Shankaracharya was the relinking of popular practice to the theory of Brahman, the stem infusion of mythological fancies with the doctrine of the Upanishads. He took up and defined the current catchwords—Maya, Karma, reincarnation, and others—and left the terminology of Hinduism what it is today. At the same time, we must not neglect to remind ourselves that in all this, if he had been other than the expression of that which it was the actual tendency of the race to formulate, he would not have found the scope he did. The recognition of a great man is as essential a factor in his history, as his own power and character. His complete appropriation by his nation only shows that he is in perfect unison with its thought and aspiration.

The two or three centuries immediately succeeding Shankaracharya are commonly known as the dark ages of Indian history. The application of the term is obscure. In what sense were these ages dark? They were centuries of chivalric dominance, and in many a Rajput line the bardic annals are still preserved that will one day enable a generation of Indian historians to read their record. Even the wars of such a period were never destructive; for, apart from their specially chivalrous character, Oriental military usage has always secured the safety of non combatants. The lives of water carriers and commissariat servants were scrupulously respected in Asiatic warfare. It is said, indeed, that the European gipsy is an example of this. These poor people were originally a tribe of petty merchants who used to accompany the march of armies. Wherever the camp was pitched, they could run up a bazaar in half an hour and their caste honour lay in telling neither side the secret's of the other. When Genghis Khan invaded Hungary, these particular clans were carried there, never to return.

But it was not only camp followers who were protected by a law, such as that which now defends the Red Cross Sisterhoods of Europe. A like consideration prevailed, with regard to the peasant working in the fields, and the craftsman toiling at his anvil. The young crops were honoured in ancient combat, as would be Cologne Cathedral or Notre Dame de Paris in modern. Under these circumstances a battle became only a deadly form of tournament, involving in its peril none but fighting men.

But if such contests could not become destructive, neither could they succeed in educating the masses of the people to the common duty of military defence. This result could only be achieved when a religious idea should become the war cry of whole regions, conferring on all men the right of struggle without distinction of caste. This right, so necessary to the completion of nationality, the Mohammedan invasion gave, and it is difficult to imagine any other way in which the lesson could have been widely learnt.

The great tide of vigour that emanated from Shankaracharya swept round India by south, west, and north, in a spiral curve. Ramanuja, Madhvacharya Ram Das and Tukaram, the Sikh Gurus and Gauranga were all in turn its products. Wherever it touched the Mussalman consciousness, it created, chiefly by means of contest, a well centred nation. Where it did not come in contact with Mohammedanism, as in the extreme south, this spiritual energy did not succeed in evoking a nationality. And where it did not lead to definite fighting, as in Bengal under Chaitanya, the sense of national existence remained more or less potential. Thus the advent of Islam into India during the post-Shankaracharyan period cannot be regarded as a revolutionary invasion, in as much as under the new power there was no loss of Asiatic modes. New arts of luxury were introduced, but the general economic system remained undisturbed. India received a more centralised government than had been possible since the Ashokan Empire, but no new forces came into operation, tending to reduce her own children to the position of agricultural serfs or tenants. And we have seen that even the wars which arose between contiguous populations of Hindus and Mohammedans must be regarded rather as those athletic contests between brothers and cousins which confer individuality, than as conquests on the one side or the other. The victor after victory attempts neither to exclude his rival's creed from office, nor to create invidious distinctions. "The great bankers and nobles of Bengal remained Hindu under the rule of the Nawabs, as naturally as the Mussalman maintained his faith in the shadow of a Hindu throne."

Nor have the clearness and self-consciousness that its definition has added to Hinduism in any way tended to impair its inclusiveness.

For the personality that the 19th century has revealed as the turningpoint of the national development is that of Ramakrishna Paramahamsa, whose name stands as another word for the synthesis of all possible ideals and all possible shades of thought. In this great life, Hinduism finds the philosophy of Shankaracharya clothed upon with flesh, and is made finally aware of the entire sufficiency of any single creed or conception to lead the soul to God as its true goal. Henceforth, it is not true that each form of life or worship is tolerated or understood by the Hindu mind; each form is justified, welcomed, set up for its passionate loving, for evermore. Henceforth, the supreme crime for the follower of any Indian sect, whether orthodox or modern, philosophic or popular, shall be the criticism of any other, as if it were without the bounds of "the Eternal Faith." "Man proceeds from truth to truth, and not from error to truth," becomes in future the formula that constitutes belief.

At this point we could almost have prophesied, had it not already happened, that some great disciple of this master would declare, on behalf of the whole nation, that the final differentia of Hinduism lay in the acceptance of the doctrine of the Ishta Devata, i.e., the right of every man to choose his own creed, and of none to force the same choice on any other.

At last, then, Indian thought stands revealed in its entirety–no sect, but a synthesis; no church, but a university of spiritual culture—as an idea of individual freedom, amongst the most complete that the world knows. Certain conceptions, such as Maya, Karma, and reincarnation, popularised by Buddhism, and Mukti or the beatific vision, sown broadcast alike by Shankaracharya and the Sufis, are characteristic of large areas. But they are nowhere and in no sense regarded as essential. For it is as foreign to the genius of Hinduism to require an oath of conformity to any given religious tenet whatever, as it would be to the habits of an Oxford don to require adherence to the doctrines of Plato as against those of Aristotle. It would thus appear that the reforming sects of the Mohammedan period and of the nineteenth century itself, have to the full as good a right to call themselves Hindu as the most orthodox priest of Shiva, or the most learned Sanskrit Pundit.

We have seen then, that it is certainly a mistake to read the history of India at any time as the account of a struggle between Hindu and Mohammedan thought, though it is a mistake which is perhaps inseparable from the European conception of the influence of faith on politics. But it cannot, on the other hand, be too clearly understood that the problem which the Indian idea has had to face, during the period between Shankaracharya and the nineteenth century, was the inclusion of the Mohammedan element in a completed nationality. From the nineteenth century onwards, it becomes the realisation of that single united nationality, amidst the vast complexity which has been the growth of ages.

It is said that nations and systems of culture fulfil special functions, as organs of humanity just as individuals fulfil special uses in the community. If this be so, it would almost appear that within the bounds of India lies one of the focal or polar points of the race. The great task of the reconciliation of opposites would seem to devolve on the peoples within this pale. It is not enough that the Mussalman should inhabit the pastoral belt, the Mongolian rest secure behind the Thian Shan, and the Aryan and Dravidian dwell peacefully side by side in the Southern peninsula. It was decreed from the beginning, it lay unavoidably in the very nature of things, that sooner or later all these should meet in the land of the Indus, and learn their mutual significance and responsibilities. Buddhism may be regarded in one aspect as simply the synthesis of Eastern Asia. Neo-Hinduism (to borrow a term which has been coined in no friendly spirit) is equally indicative of a place found in Aryan thought for Semitic formulae, and who shall say what is yet to be born of that conjunction between all these, in which Asia shall find herself to be—not, as she has so long been told, "merely a congeries of geographical fragments," still less a concert of rival political units, held in mechanical combination by a due admixture of mutual hopes and recriminations, but a single immense organism, filled with the tide of one strong pulsating life from end to end, firm rooted in the soil of common origins and common modes? The value which we may attach to the prospect of this future will depend on the idea that we have already been able to form, of the place of Asia in the evolution of humanity, but to those who foresee a future moralisation of international relations, it may well appear that this question is among the most important questions in the world.

...This is the illumination that India calls the knowledge of unity, and the gradual appropriation of it by the whole nature, so that it ceases to be mere words and becomes a living actuality, called realisation. Thus every step, every movement in life is either dull and dead, or on fire with the growing knowledge that we know as spirituality. The highest genius becomes only an incident on the road to supreme blessedness. And the passionless desire of Pheidias that wrought Olympian Zeus, the love of Dante for Beatrice, the "glorious nothingness" of S. Teresa, and the light on the face of Faraday the physicist, are all alike and all equally beads on that rosary where the soul's experience is told. For the whole story in all its forms is summed up, to Indian thinking, in the struggle to pass from the perceiving of manifoldness to the perceiving of One, and every heightening of common knowledge is to be regarded as a step towards this. The kitten at play will pursue first one object and then another with all the bewilderment and disconnectedness of the animal mind, while even the youngest baby will show the superiority of human faculty by its greater persistence of purpose and pertinacity of desire. The man of low type is led hither and thither by every impulse of sensation, while Archimedes is so absorbed in thought that he never perceives the Roman enter his presence, nor dreams of begging more than time to finish his speculation.

It must be remembered that to the Eastern intellect, man himself is the universe, for all differentiation is within the mind. India may accept, as a working hypothesis, the theory that sociology is the synthesis of all the sciences, but her own fundamental conviction is that psychology occupies this place. Hence, to her, power is always lodged in the personality. Mind is the lord of body, undoubtedly; but mind, like body, is only the tool of the great Self of Things that stands behind and uses both for its own purpose. Like a strangely complex telescope, one part of the instrument stands pointed to give reports of many kinds of light, sound, weight, smell, taste, and touch; and by another we are led to conceive of vast ranges of these, outside the possibilities of our immediately perceiving, by which we can build up the conception that we call the Cosmos. But, according to Indian thinking again, perfect control over the apparatus has only been attained when every part of it can be directed at will to a common point—the whole power of investigation brought to bear on any object. When this is done, when the intensest vibration of the whole being is reached and every faculty is convergent on the point of attention, then declares India, we, being one, perceive oneness, the mind sees truth face to face.

How we shall interpret and express the vision is determined wholly by our own past language and discipline. The mother comes out of it to love and serve; Joan of Arc commands armies with unfaltering insight; Sir Isaac Newton gives us the law of gravitation; Mozart produces his Requiem Mass, and the Messiah comes down from the mountain side whispering, "I and My Father are One." That is to say, the selflimited joys of sense have given way to the pursuit of the good of others as an end in itself. The man is overpowered by a beauty and a truth that he must needs share with the whole world. Or the finite personality is completed, transcended in union, with the absolute and universal.

There are thus, as the East counts, two modes of existence– one the personal, or egoistic, and the other the impersonal, or supra personal, where egoism and altruism are alike forgotten. The realisation of this illimitable existence is itself salvation, and is to be reached in life, not death. Concentration is its single secret, and real power is always power over oneself.

What, then, are the common hindrances to this centring of thought and feeling that we are not all constantly immersed in the

Divine intoxication? And what are the paths by which we are ordinarily led to overcome such hindrances? For it is to be supposed that, if the experience be authentic, men first stumbled upon it by accident, and formulation of theory came afterwards.

The mind of man sweeps an infinite circle, and from every point upon the immeasurable circumference runs a life path to the vision of Unity as the common centre. Each man is, as it were, a new window through which all others may look upon the Infinite, each life a new name for That which we call God. The paths, therefore, are countless. No two methods can be exactly the same. Yet there are certain broad characteristics which are more or less general.

The soul that thirsts for service, gradually expunging from the area of motive even the subtler shades of selfishness—such as the preference for special forms of activity, exactingness on behalf of work, and desire for sympathy and affection as the result—this soul will more readily than another lose itself in the supreme intuition of the good of others. "The People" with Mazzini, "the fair realm of France" with Joan of Arc, the fulfilment of duty to his country with the great sovereign or statesman, are amongst the forms which this realisation takes. In such a mood of uttermost blessedness, some have even suffered death by fire.

The temporary experience, in which the subject becomes unconscious of bodily sensation, is called *Samadhi*. The process by which he comes out of *Samadhi* time after time, to work its volume of force, so to speak, into his daily life, is known as realisation. And the path of service in purity of motive, is spoken of as Karma-yoga, or divine union by work.

Again, we can in some measure understand the development of a nature to whom everything appears in degrees of lovableness. This was undoubtedly the method of S. Francis, and alter him of S. Teresa. It is called in India Bhakti, or devotion. Gradually, in such souls—guided by the thought of reaching the Infinite in abnegation of self—the power of love becomes a fire scorching, burning, consuming the barriers of individuality. "One cannot understand," says S. Teresa, "what is meant by talking of the impermanence of worldly joys. For one would renounce them so much the more gladly, could they but be eternal." Then there is a fusing of all things in the one conception of the beloved. Lastly, distinction ceases, self is forgotten, there is left nothing, save the Infinite Love. First the prayer of quiet, then the prayer of union, last the irresistible rapture, says the great Carmelite. Such is Bhakti-yoga, the road by which the vast majority of the saints have gone.

Highest of all, however, is Union by knowledge or *Jnanayoga*. A life whose whole struggle is the passion for truth; a soul to which falsehood or superstition is the worst of sins; a mind clear as the black depths of a mountain pool; an atmosphere of joy, all stillness, all calm, all radiance without emotion; to these comes the growing intensity of recognition, the increasing power of direct vision, and finally that last illumination, in which there is neither knower, knowing nor known, but all is one in Oneness. It is much to be regretted that we have in English no word corresponding to Jnana. Insight has a certain affinity, but is not sufficiently intense. The fact is, the habit of thought that leads up to the conception is foreign to us: a true parallelism is, therefore, out of the question.

The greatest Jnani that has appeared in human history was undoubtedly Buddha, for the calmness of intellect predominates in Him, living through a ministry of more than forty years, though it was the immense outburst of His love and pity (explained as the fruit of five hundred sacrifices of Himself) that drove Him forth on His passionate quest to serve mankind. Then He is also in a high degree a combination of the three types of realisation—by intellect, heart and work. Some measure of this amalgamation there must be in all who use their knowledge for the good of others, of whom the incarnations are the culminating type. For in Jnana by itself, the personal existence is seen to be a dream, a mere illusion, and it is impossible for him, who has once received its overwhelming revelation, to believe that there exist outside himself other centres of illusion for whose emancipation he might work.

For karma, or service, again, there could be no sufficient motive, without the impulse of Bhakti. And the madness of divine love, unlighted by knowledge, unawaking to compassion, is almost unthinkable.

Such are the three ways—truth, devotion, and good works—by which it is said that souls may reach their goal. He who has attained, and remains in life, is called a *Paramahamsa*, or swan amongst men. And of all such, Shuka—he to whom it was given while in mortal form to drink a handful of the waters of the ocean of superconsciousness—is ideal and head. For most men die, it has been said, having heard only the thunder of its waves upon the shore; a few come within sight; fewer still taste; to Shuka alone was it given to drink. Many Mohammedan saints have become Paramahamsas, and are equally loved and reverenced by all religions alike.

So far of the apprehension of unity when consciousness and selfdirection have made it vital spirituality. The hindrance to our reaching it is always, it is declared, one, namely, under whatever guise, want of the power to give up self. "When desire is gone, and all the cords of the heart are broken, then," says the Upanishad, "a man attains to immortality." And by "immortality," it should be understood, is here meant the quality of deathlessness. For this reason, all religions are a call to renunciation; all ethics negate selfishness of personality; all disciplines are a repression of individual impulse. In the Indian doctrine of one immanent in the many, all these receive interpretation. The scholar's austerity of study; the artist's striving to become the witness; the lover's desire to sacrifice himself; all speak, however unconsciously, of our longing not to be, that the infinite, the universal consciousness, may abide within us.

The fact that the final achievement is variously known as Freedom, Mukti, or Nirvana, the annihilation of the limited, requires, at this point, little explanation. The idea that the perception of manifoldness is Maya or illusion, that the One is the real, and the many unreal, underlies the whole theory. "They that behold the One in all the changing manifoldness of this universe, unto them belongs eternal peace—unto none else, unto none else."

Obviously, the final truth of the doctrine is capable of no other proof or disproof than that of experience. But the attitude to it of the common Indian mind is strictly scientific. We cannot prove, save by making the experiment, but we can point to the fact that the accumulated observation of life goes to establish the tenableness of the proposition, says India in effect. And when we are shown one morality that does not demand the holding of unity of principle against manifoldness of impulse; one science that does not grow by the correlating of apparent discrepancies in continually stricter unities; or one character that does not find perfection in surrendering the personal to the impersonal, the theory of Maya—real unity amidst apparent diversity—will fall to the ground, and must be acknowledged a misconception. Hitherto, it may be claimed, the whole history of the world has not sufficed to furnish the required exception.

Thus the beatific vision of Hinduism is not unlike that of Dante's Empyrean, only it is to be relegated to no distant future, but triumphantly vindicated within mortality itself. The name of God and the conventions of piety are as unreal as anything else in Maya, but they have the power of enabling us to break its bondage, whereas the delights of the senses only fasten it the tighter.

One point remains. The doctrine with which we have been dealing represents a national culture. Very few in the west can be said to have grasped the whole secret of that for which their country stands. Very few will be found to understand deeply any given idea or subject. The very reverse is the case in the East. Men who have no emancipation into the scheme of modern knowledge are emancipated into the sequence of renunciation and freedom. Though India is daily losing her grip on her own character, she is still the motherland of hundreds of the saints. And amongst that people of ancient aristocracies the realm of the ideal is so completely democratised that the poorest peasant, the meanest workman, comprehends what is meant by the great daily prayer of Hinduism: —

From the unreal, lead us to the Real!
From darkness, lead us unto Light!
From death, lead us to Immortality!
Reach us through and through ourself,
And evermore protect us—O Thou Terrible!—
From ignorance by Thy sweet compassionate Face.

...I had, before my departure for Europe, the great privilege of living in a simple Indian home, making Indian friends, and being taught in some measure to act and think and feel like an Indian woman. I lay stress upon the fact that it was not amongst the rich and great that my lines were cast. For the life that I was thus allowed to share was that of the common Indian world. Bengali in its details, it was in its main features that of the masses of the people the country over. And this I know because in the Himalayas, being allowed to join in a great pilgrimage, I saw, amongst people from all the provinces of India, that same quiet simple life, that same passionate reverence for purity, that some sense of the sacramental significance of food, the same depth of thought and feeling that formed the characteristic elements of the daily routine in my Calcutta home.

It was this memory, then, of a household of orthodox Hindu women that I carried with me during my recent wanderings amidst the luxury and splendour of the west. It is this memory that I bring back to you today undimmed, and that prompts me to say to you what I have found to be the truth.

Just as it has been realised already that in religion you have a great deal to give, and nothing to learn from the west, so also in social matters it will be well to understand that what changes are necessary you are fully competent to make for yourselves, and no outside has the right to advise or interfere. Changes no doubt there will be. Change is probably inseparable from the process of life. But these changes must be original, selfdetermined, selfwrought. What! does the civilisation of three thousand years mean nothing that the young nations of the west should be in a position to lead the peoples of the east?

They tell us that India wants civilising, that Indian life is barbarous. Nay, we answer, it is simple, but this simplicity resembles the religious thought of India in being itself not only a special form of civilisation of a very high order, but in also providing the solution of the abstract and universal problem of all civilisations. For, you have devised a scheme of life which leaves the refinement of the individual intact, though all wealth be taken from him. Under all other forms known to me, good breeding diminishes with loss of means. The rich man is distinctly more civilised than the poor can ever be. The aristocrat who drops into the lower ranks loses his selfrespect more miserably than any. Here these things are not so. And why not so? Because before Europe was born, India had grasped the essential fact that the end of civilisation lies in the making of men—not wealth, not power, not organisation.

When we have said that a country contains twenty millions, and twenty million employees, we have said a terrible thing, no matter what the glory and wealth of that country may seem to be. When we have said that in another country the beggar is worshipped, we have not yet said anything of importance. But when one is able to state that the civilisation of a people is a great ladder by which every man and woman of that people is striving to mount to a higher selfdevelopment, a greater culture, a broader outlook, one has reached the utmost that can be said of any nation.

I am far from desiring to flatter my audience. I am anxious to leave individuals entirely on one side. But I must be allowed to confess that as I look at the inner trend of Indian life, as I realise on the one hand the fact that Gautama Buddha is the national type according to which all individuals must be measured, and on the other hand your readiness to translate and reapply the great vision of the Bo-tree into any form of learning—saying for instance—"Perfect music is Samadhi"—I am puzzled as to whether Christianity is to be regarded as par excellence the Asiatic Mission in the west, or whether we must not add the University to the Church, in order to complete the statement.

For the problems on which India was engaged when she was overtaken by what we may call the modern epoch, were not lower, but higher than the problems proper to that epoch. She succumbed because the student absorbed in his mathematics may be less fit to deal with the outside world than some far lower type of man in the street, and may succumb.

They say that Indian women are ignorant and oppressed. To all who make this statement we may answer that Indian women are certainly not oppressed. The crime of illtreating women is at once less common and less brutal in form here than in younger countries. And the happiness, the social importance, and may I say, the lofty character of Indian women are amongst the grandest possessions of the national life.

When we come to the charge that Indian women are ignorant, we meet with a far deeper fallacy. They are ignorant in the modern form, that is to say, few can write, and not very many can read. Are they then illiterate? If so, the Mahabharata and the Ramayana and the Puranas and stories every mother and every grandmother tells to the babies, are not Literature. But European novels and the Strand Magazine by the same token are? Can any of us accept this paradox?

The fact is, writing is not culture though it is an occasional result of culture. The greatest literature occurs at the beginning of a literary age and so, to those who know Indian life, it is easy to see that an Indian woman who has the education of the Indian home, the dignity, the gentleness, the cleanliness, the thrift, the religious training, the culture of mind and heart, which that homelife entails, though she cannot perhaps read a word of her own language, much less sign her name, may be infinitely better educated in every true sense, and in the literary sense also, than her glib critic.

The remaining charge that seems to me of a grave enough nature to require reply is that out yonder on the quays and in your streets are your pariahs, your outcastes, and that to touch these people seems to be such defilement that you have deliberately added to their degradation and unhappiness through unnumbered ages.

My friends, if this statement was true, that you had really lived amongst these poor aborigines in this fashion, then I could only say, that you had been guilty of living in the country like foreigners, with the feeling of foreigners. And from India herself I have learnt that to feel as a foreigner is always vulgar. But in this case again, whatever the faults of individuals may have been, and it is possible because they are men, the inner trend of the great civilisation that has grown up on this different soil is something very different.

There is nothing that Hinduism has recognised so clearly as the need to Hinduism of the lowest castes, and the world owes eternal gratitude to the race that has held out a system of life in which rank was a sign, a synonym for cleanliness and care about food, and in which these luxurious purities were made subordinate to the conscious aim of increasing brain power, and emotional power and selfcontrol. We must never forget that to make every man and woman into a Rama or a Sita or a Gautama Buddha is the strenuous purpose of Indian culture, and the very pariah who recognises this standard as the supreme test, is higher by that fact than the man who imagines his possession of wealth or beauty or a throne to be anything in itself. So much for the past. Now for the present and for the future.

4

Collection from the Complete Works of Sri Aurobindo

...When we look at the past of India, what strikes us is her stupendous vitality, her inexhaustible power of life and joy of life, her almost unimaginably prolific creativeness. For three thousand years at least, it is indeed much longer, she has been creating abundantly and incessantly, lavishly, with an inexhaustible many-sidedness, republics and kingdoms and empires, philosophies and cosmogonies and sciences and creeds and arts and poems and all kinds of monuments, palaces and temples and public works, communities and societies and religious orders, laws and codes and rituals, physical sciences, psychic sciences, systems of Yoga, systems of politics and administration, arts spiritual, arts worldly, trades, industries, fine crafts, the list is endless and in each item there is almost a plethora of activity. She creates and creates and is not satisfied and is not tired; she will not have an end of it, seems hardly to need a space for rest, a time for inertia and lying fallow. She expands too outside her borders; her ships cross the ocean and the fine superfluity of her wealth brims over of Judea and Egypt and Rome; her traces are found in the sands of Mesopotamia; her religions conquer China and Japan and spread westward as far as Palestine and Alexandria, and the figures of the Upanishads and the sayings of the Buddhists are reechoed on the lips of Christ. Everywhere, as on her soil, so in her works there is the teeming of a superabundant energy of life...

Indeed without this opulent vitality and opulent intellectuality India could never have done so much as she did with her spiritual tendencies. It is a great error to suppose the spirituality flourishes best in an impoverished soil with the life half killed and the intellect discouraged and intimidated. The spirituality that so flourishes is something morbid, hectic and exposed to perilous reactions. It is when the race has lived most richly and thought most profoundly that spirituality finds its heights and its depths and its constant and many sided fruition.

...The religious culture which now goes by the name of Hinduism.......gave itself no name, because it set itself no sectarian limits; it claimed no universal adhesion, asserted no sole infallible dogma, set up no single narrow path or gate of salvation; it was less a creed or cult than a continuously enlarging tradition of the Godward endeavour of the human spirit. An immense many sided and many staged provision for a spiritual selfbuilding and selffinding, it had some right to speak of itself by the only name it knew, the eternal religion, sanatana dharma...

...Indian philosophy has led away from the study of nature is to state a gross unfact and to ignore the magnificent history of Indian civilisation. If by nature is meant physical nature, the plain truth is that no nation before the modern epoch carried scientific research so far and with such signal success as India of ancient times. That is a truth which lies on the face of history for all to read; it has been brought forward with great force and much wealth of detail by Indian scholars and scientists of higher eminence, but it was already known and acknowledged by European savants who had taken the trouble to make a comparative study in the subject. Not only was India in the first rank in mathematics, astronomy, chemistry, medicine, surgery, all the branches of physical knowledge which were practiced in ancient times, but she was, along with the Greeks, the teacher of the Arabs from whom Europe recovered the lost habit of scientific enquiry and got the basis from which modern science started. In many directions India had the priority of discovery, to take only two striking examples among a multitude, the decimal notation in mathematics or the perception that the earth is a moving body in astronomy, *cala prthvi sthira bhati*, the earth moves and only appears to be still, said the Indian astronomer many centuries before Galileo.

...This great and ancient nation was once the fountain of human light, the apex of human civilisation, the examplar of courage and humanity, the perfection of good Government and settled society, the mother of all religions, the teacher of all wisdom and philosophy. It has suffered much at the hands of inferior civilisations and more savage peoples; it has gone down into the shadow of night and tasted often of the bitterness of death. Its pride has been trampled into the dust and its glory has departed. Hunger and misery and despair have become the masters of this fair soil, these noble hills, these ancient rivers, these cities whose life story goes back into prehistoric night. But do you think that therefore God has utterly abandoned us and given us up for ever to be a mere convenience for the west, the helots of its commerce, and the feeders of its luxury and pride? We are still God's chosen people and all our calamities have been but a discipline of suffering, because for the great mission before us prosperity was not sufficient, adversity had also its training; to taste the glory of power and beneficence and joy was not sufficient, the knowledge of weakness and torture and humiliation was also needed; it was not enough that we should be able to fill the role of the merciful sage and the beneficent king, we had also to experience in our own persons the feelings of the outcaste and the slave.

...We can reply on the cultural issue from the viewpoint of the past and the valuation of different cultures as acquired contributions to the growth of the human race, that Indian civilisation has been the form and expression of a culture as great as any of the historic civilisations of mankind, great in religion, great in philosophy, great in science, great in thought of many kinds, great in literature, art and poetry, great in the organisation of society and politics, great in craft and trade and commerce. There have been dark spots, positive imperfections, heavy shortcomings; what civilisation has been perfect, which has not had its deep stains and cruel abysses? There have been considerable lacunae, many blind alleys, much uncultured or illcultured ground: what civilisation has been without its unfilled parts, its negative aspects? But our ancient civilisation can survive the severest comparisons of cither ancient or mediaeval times. More highreaching, subtle, many sided, curious and profound than the Greek, more noble and humane than the Roman, more large and spiritual than the old Egyptian, more vast and original than any other Asiatic civilisation, more intellectual than the European prior to the eighteenth century, possessing all that these had and more, it was the most powerful, selfpossessed, stimulating and wide in influence of all past human cultures.

And if we look from the viewpoint of the present and the fruitful workings of the progressive Time-Spirit, we can say that even here in spite of our downfall all is not on the debit side. Many of the forms of our civilisation have become inapt and effete and others stand in need of radical change and renovation. But that can be said equally well of European culture; for all its recently acquired progressiveness and habit of more rapid selfadaptation, large parts of it are already rotten and out of date. In spite of all drawbacks and in spite of downfall the spirit of Indian culture, its central ideas, its best ideals have still their message for humanity and not for India alone. And we in India hold that they are capable of developing out of themselves by contact with new need and idea as good and better solutions of the problems before us than those which are offered to us secondhand from Western sources. But besides the comparisons of the past and the needs of the present there is too a viewpoint of the ideal future. There are the farther goals towards which humanity is moving, and the present is only a crude aspiration towards them and the immediate future we now see in hope and strive to bring about in form, only its crude preparatory stage. There is an unrealised standard of the ideas which to the mind of the moment are figments of Utopia, but may become to a more developed humanity the commonplaces of their daily environment, the familiar things of the present which they have to overpass. How stands Indian civilisation with regard to this yet unrealised future of the race? Are its master ideas and dominant powers guiding lights or helping forces towards it or do they end in themselves with no vistas on the evolutionary potentialities of the earth's coming ages?

The very idea of progress is an illusion to some minds; for they imagine that the race moves constantly in a circle. Or even their view is that greatness more often than not is to be found in the past and that the line of our movement is a curve of deterioration, a downward lapse. But that is an illusion created when we look too much upon the highlights of the past and forget its shadows or concentrate too much on the dark spaces of the present and ignore its powers of light and its aspects of happier promise. It is created too by a mistaken deduction from the phenomenon of an uneven progress. For nature effects her evolution through a rhythm of advance and relapse, day and night, waking and sleep; there is a temporary pushing of certain results at the expense of others not less desirable for perfection and to a superficial eye there may seem to be a relapse even in our advance. Progress admittedly does not march on securely in a straight line like a man sure of his familiar way or an army covering an unimpeded terrain or wellmapped unoccupied spaces. Human progress is very much an adventure through the unknown, an unknown full of surprises and baffling obstacles; it stumbles often, it misses its way at many points, it cedes here in order to gain there, it retraces its steps frequently in order to get more widely forward. The present does not always compare favourably with the past; even when it is more advanced in the mass, it may still be inferior in certain directions important to our inner or our outer welfare. But earth does move forward after all, *eppur si muove*. Even in failure there is a preparation for success: our nights carry in them the secret of a greater dawn. This is a frequent experience in our individual progress, but the human collectivity also moves in much the same manner. The question is whither are we marching or what are the true routes and harbours of our voyage.

Western civilisation is proud of its successful modernism. But there is much that it has lost in the eagerness of its gains and much which men of old strove towards that it has not even attempted to accomplish. There is much too that it has willfully flung aside in impatience or scorn to its own great loss, to the injury of its life, to the imperfection of its culture. An ancient Greek of the time of Pericles or the philosophers suddenly transported in time to this century would be astonished by the immense gains of the intellect and the expansion of the mind, the modern manysidedness of the reason and inexhaustible habit of inquiry, the power of endless generalisation and precise detail. He would admire without reserve the miraculous growth of science and its giant discoveries, the abundant power, richness and minuteness of its instrumentation, the wonder working force of its inventive genius. He would be overcome and stupefied rather than surprised and charmed by the enormous stir and pulsation of modern life. But at the same time he would draw back repelled from its unashamed mass of ugliness and vulgarity, its unchastened external utilitarianism, its vitalistic riot and the morbid exaggeration and unsoundness of many of its growths. He would see in it much illdisguised evidence of the uneliminated survival of the triumphant barbarian. If he recognised its intellectuality and the scrupulous application of thought and scientific reason to the machinery of life, he would miss in it his own later attempt at the clear and noble application of the ideal reason to the inner life of the mind and the soul. He would find that in this civilisation beauty had become an exotic and the shining ideal mind in some fields a debased and exploited slave and in others a neglected stranger. As for the great spiritual seekers of the past, they would experience in all this huge activity of the intellect and the life the sense of an aching void. A feeling of its illusion and unreality because that which is greatest in man and raises him beyond himself had been neglected, would oppress them at every step. The discovery of the laws of physical Nature would not compensate in their eyes for the comparative decline for a long time it was the almost absolute cessation of a greater seeking and finding, the discovery of the freedom of the spirit.

But an unbiassed view will prefer to regard this age of civilisation as an evolutionary stage, an imperfect but important turn of the human advance. It is then possible to see that great gains have been made which are of the utmost value to an ultimate perfection, even if they have been made at a great price. There is not only a greater generalisation of knowledge and more thorough use of intellectual power and activity in multiple fields. There is not only the advance of Science and its application to the conquest of our environment, an immense apparatus of means, vast utilisations, endless minute conveniences, an irresistible machinery, a tireless exploitation of forces. There is too a certain development of powerful if not high pitched ideals and there is an attempt, however external and therefore imperfect, to bring them to bear upon the working of human society as a whole. Much has been diminished or lost, but it can be recovered, eventually, if not with ease. Once restored to its true movement, the inner life of man will find that it has gained in materials, in power of plasticity, in a new kind of depth and wideness. And we shall have acquired a salutary habit of manysided thoroughness and a sincere endeavour to shape the outer collective life into an adequate image of our highest ideals. Temporary diminutions will not count before the greater inner expansion that is likely to succeed this age of external turmoil and outward looking endeavour.

If on the other hand an ancient Indian of the time of the Upanishads, the Buddhist period or the later classical age were to be set down in modern India and note that larger part of its life which belongs to the age of decline, he would experience a much more depressing sensation, the sense of a national, a cultural debacle, a fall from the highest summits to discouragingly low levels. He might well ask himself what this degenerate posterity had done with the mighty civilisation of the past. He would wonder how with so much to inspire, to elevate, to spur them to yet greater accomplishment and selfexceeding, they could have lapsed into this impotent and inert confusion and, instead of developing the high motives of Indian culture to yet deeper and wider issues, allowed them to overload themselves with ugly accretions, to rust, to rot, almost to perish. He would see his race clinging to forms and shells and rags of the past and missing nine-tenths of its nobler values. He would compare the spiritual light and energy of the heroic ages of the Upanishads and the philosophies with the later inertia or small and broken fragmentarily derivative activity of our philosophic thought. After the intellectual curiosity, the scientific development, the creative literary and artistic greatness, the noble fecundity of the classical age he would be amazed by the extent of a later degeneracy, its mental poverty, immobility, static repetition, the comparative feebleness of the creative intuition, the long sterility of art, the cessation of science. He would deplore a prone descent to ignorance, a failing of the old powerful will and tapasya, almost a volitional impotence. In place of the simpler and more spiritually rational order of old times he would find a bewildering chaotic disorganised organisation of things without centre and without any large harmonising idea. He would find not a true social order but a half arrested, half hastening putrescence. In place of the great adaptable civilisation which assimilated with power and was able to return tenfold for what it received, he would meet a helplessness that bore passively or only with a few ineffectual galvanic reactions the forces of the outside world and the stress of adverse circumstance. At one time he would see that there had been even a loss of faith and selfconfidence so considerable as to tempt the intellectuals of the nation to scrap the ancient spirit and ideals for an alien and imported culture. He would note indeed the beginning of a change, but might perhaps doubt how deep it had gone or whether it was powerful enough to save, forceful enough to upheave the whole nation from its cherished torpor and weakness, enlightened enough to guide a new and robust creative activity towards the building of new significant forms for the ancient spirit.

Here too a better understanding points to hope rather than to the flat despondency suggested by a too hasty surface glance. This last age of Indian history is an example of the constant local succession of night even to the most long and brilliant day in the evolution of the race. But it was a night filled at first with many and brilliant constellations and even at its thickest and worst it was the darkness of Kalidasa's *viceya-taraka prabhata-kalpeva sarvari*, "night preparing for dawn, with a few just decipherable stars." Even in the decline all was not loss; there were needed developments, there were spiritual and other gains of the greatest importance for the future. If the high spiritualised mind and stupendous force of spiritual will, *tapasya*, that characterised ancient India were less in evidence, there were new gains of spiritual emotion and sensitiveness to spiritual impulse on the lower planes of consciousness, that had been lacking before. Architecture, literature, painting, sculpture lost the grandeur, power, nobility of old, but evoked other powers and motives full of delicacy, vividness and grace. There was a descent from the heights to the lower levels, but a descent that gathered riches on its way and was needed for the fullness of spiritual discovery and experience. And in the worst period of decline and failure the spirit was not dead in India, but only torpid, concealed and shackled; now emerging in answer to a pressure of constant awakening shocks for a strong selfliberation it finds that its sleep was a preparation of new potentialities behind the veil of that slumber. The decline of our past culture may even be regarded as a needed waning and dying of old forms to make way not only for a new, but, if we will that it should be so, a greater and more perfect creation.

For after all it is the will in the being that gives to circumstances their value, and often an unexpected value; the hue of apparent actuality is a misleading indicator. If the will in a race or civilisation is towards death, if it clings to the lassitude of decay and the laissez faire of the moribund or even in strength insists blindly upon the propensities that lead to destruction or if it cherishes only the powers of dead Time and puts away from it the powers of the future, if it prefers life that was to life that will be, nothing, not even abundant strength and resources and intelligence, not even many calls to live and constantly offered opportunities will save it from an inevitable disintegration or collapse. But if there comes to it a strong faith in itself and a robust will to live, if it is open to the things that shall come, willing to seize on the future and what it offers and strong to compel it where it seems adverse, it can draw from adversity and defeat a force of invincible victory and rise from apparent helplessness and decay in a mighty flame of renovation to the light of a more splendid life. This is what Indian civilisation is now rearising to do as it has always done in the eternal strength of its spirit.

The greatness of the ideals of the past is a promise of greater ideals for the future. A continual expansion of what stood behind past endeavour and capacity is the one abiding justification of a living culture. But it follows that civilisation and barbarism are words of a quite relative significance. For from the view of the evolutionary future European and Indian civilisation at their best have only been half achievements, infant dawns pointing to the mature sunlight that is to come. Neither Europe nor India nor any race, country or continent of mankind has ever been fully civilised from this point of view; none has grasped the whole secret of a true and perfect human living, none has applied with an entire insight or a perfectly vigilant sincerity even the little they were able to achieve. If we define civilisation as a harmony of spirit, mind and body, where has that harmony been entire or altogether real? Where have there not been glaring deficiencies and painful discords? Where has the whole secret of the harmony been altogether grasped in all its parts or the complete music of life evolved into the triumphant ease of a satisfying, durable and steadily mounting concord? Not only are there everywhere positive, ugly, even "hideous" blots on the life of man, but much that we now accept with equanimity, much in which we take pride, may well be regarded by a future humanity as barbarism or at least as semibarbarous and immature. The achievements that we regard as ideal, will be condemned as a selfsatisfied imperfection blind to its own errors; the ideas that we vaunt as enlightenment will appear as a demilight or a darkness. Not only will many forms of our life that claim to be ancient or even eternal, as if that could be said of any form of things, fail and disappear; the subjective shapes given to our best principles and ideals will perhaps claim from the future at best an understanding indulgence. There is little that will not have to undergo expansion and mutation, change perhaps beyond recognition or accept to be modified in a new synthesis. In the end the coming ages may look on Europe and Asia of today much as we look on savage tribes or primitive peoples. And this view from the future, if we can get it, is undoubtedly the most illuminating and dynamic standpoint from which we can judge our present; but it does not invalidate our comparative appreciation of past and extant cultures.

For this past and present are creating the greater steps of that future and much of it will survive even in that which supplants it. There is behind our imperfect cultural figures a permanent spirit to which we must cling and which will remain permanent even hereafter; there are certain fundamental motives or essential idea forces which cannot be thrown aside, because they are part of the vital principle of our being and of the aim of Nature in us, our svadharma. But these motives, these idea forces are, whether for nation or for humanity as a whole, few and simple in their essence and capable of an application always varying and progressive. The rest belongs to the less internal layers of our being and must undergo the changing pressure and satisfy the forward moving demands of the Time Spirit. There is this permanent spirit in things and there is this persistent swadharma or law of our nature; but there is too a less binding system of laws of successive formulation,—rhythms of the spirit, forms, turns, habits of the nature, and these endure the mutations of the ages, yugadharma. The race must obey this double principle of persistence and mutation or bear the penalty of a decay and deterioration that may attaint even its living centre.

Certainly we must repel with vigour every disintegrating or injurious attack; but it is much more important to form our own true and independent view of our own past achievement, present position and future possibilities, what we were, what we are and what we may be. In our past we must distinguish all that was great, essential, elevating, vitalising, illuminating, victorious, effective. And in that again we must distinguish what was close to the permanent, essential spirit and the persistent law of our cultural being and separate from it what was temporary and transiently formulative. For all that was great in the past cannot be preserved as it was or repeated for ever; there are new needs, there are other vistas before us. But we have to distinguish too what was deficient, illgrasped, imperfectly formulated or only suited to the limiting needs of the age or unfavourable circumstances. For it is quite idle to pretend that all in the past, even at its greatest, was entirely admirable and in its kind the highest consummate achievement of the human mind and spirit. Afterwards we have to make a comparison of this past with our present and to understand the causes of our decline and seek the remedy of our shortcomings and ailments. Our sense of the greatness of our past must not be made a fatally hypnotising lure to inertia; it should be rather an inspiration to renewed and greater achievement. But in our criticism of the present we must not be onesided or condemn with a foolish impartiality all that we are or have done. Neither flattering or glossing over our downfall nor fouling our nest to win the applause of the stranger, we have to note our actual weakness and its roots, but to fix too our eyes with a still firmer attention on our elements of strength, our abiding potentialities, our dynamic impulses of selfrenewal.

A second comparison has to be made between the west and India. In the past of Europe and the past of India we can observe with an unbiassed mind the successes of the West, the gifts it brought to humanity, but also its large gaps, striking deficiencies, terrible and even "hideous" vices and failures. On the other balance we have to cast ancient and mediaeval India's achievements and failures. Here we shall find that there is little for which we need lower our heads before Europe and much in which we rise well and sometimes immeasurably above her. But we have to scrutinise next the present of the West in its strong success, vitality, conquering insolence. What has been great in it we shall allow, but take deep note too of its defects, stumblings and dangers. And with this dangerous greatness we must compare the present of India, her downfall and its causes, her velleities of revival, her elements that still make for superiority now and in the future. Let us see and take account of all that we must inevitably receive from the west and consider how we can assimilate it to our own spirit and ideals. But let us see too what founts of native power there are in ourselves from which we can draw deeper, more vital and fresher streams of the power of life than from anything the west can offer. For that will help us more than occidental forms and motives, because it will be more natural to us, more stimulating to our idiosyncrasy of nature, more packed with creative suggestions, more easily taken up and completely followed in power of practice.

But far more helpful than any of these necessary comparisons will be the forward look from our past and present towards our own and not any foreign ideal of the future. For it is our evolutionary push towards the future that will give to our past and present their true value and significance. India's nature, her mission, the work that she has to do, her part in the earth's destiny, the peculiar power for which she stands is written there in her past history and is the secret purpose behind her present sufferings and ordeals. A reshaping of the forms of our spirit will have to take place; but it is the spirit itself behind past forms that we have to disengage and preserve and to give to it new and powerful thought significances, culture values, a new instrumentation, greater figures. And so long as we recognise these essential things and are faithful to their spirit, it will not hurt us to make even the most drastic mental or physical adaptations and the most extreme cultural and social changes. But these changes themselves must be cast in the spirit and mould of India and not in any other, not in the spirit of America or Europe, not in the mould of Japan or Russia. We must recognise the great gulf between what we are and what we may and ought to strive to be. But this we must do not in any spirit of discouragement or denial of ourselves and the truth of our spirit, but in order to measure the advance we have to make. For we have to find its true lines and to find in ourselves the aspiration and inspiration, the fire and the force to conceive them and to execute.

An original truth seeking thought is needed if we are to take this stand and make this movement, a strong and courageous intuition, an unfailing spiritual and intellectual rectitude. The courage to defend our culture against ignorant occidental criticism and to maintain it against the gigantic modern pressure comes first, but with it there must be the courage to admit not from any European standpoint but from our own outlook the errors of our culture. Apart from all phenomena of decline or deterioration, we should recognise without any sophistical denial those things in our creeds of life and social institutions which are in themselves mistaken and some of them indefensible, things weakening to our national life, degrading to our civilisation, dishonouring to our culture. A flagrant example can be found in the treatment of our outcastes. There are those who would excuse it as an unavoidable error in the circumstances of the past; there are others who contend that it was the best possible solution then available. There are still others who would justify it and, with whatever modifications, prolong it as necessary to our social synthesis. The contention is highly disputable. The excuse was there, but it is no justification for continuance. A solution which condemns by segregation one sixth of the nation to permanent ignominy, continued filth, uncleanliness of the inner and outer life and a brutal animal existence instead of lifting them out of it is no solution but rather an acceptance of weakness and a constant wound to the social body and to its collective spiritual, intellectual, moral and material welfare. A social synthesis which can only live by making a permanent rule of the degradation of our fellowmen and countrymen stands condemned and foredoomed to decay and disturbance. The evil effects may be kept under for a long time and work only by the subtler unobserved action of the law of Karma; but once the light of Truth is let in on these dark spots, to perpetuate them is to maintain a seed of disruption and ruin our chances of eventual survival.

Again, we have to look on our cultural ideas and our social forms and see where they have lost their ancient spirit or real significance. Many of them are now a fiction and no longer in accordance with the ideas they assume or with the facts of life. Others even if good in themselves or else beneficent in their own time are no longer sufficient for our growth. All these must either be transformed or discarded and truer ideas and better formulations must be found in their place. The new turn we must give them will not always be a return upon their old significance. The new dynamic truths we have to discover need not be parked within the limited truth of a past ideal. On our past and present ideals we have to turn the searchlight of the spirit and see whether they have not to be surpassed or enlarged or brought into consonance with new wider ideals. All we do or create must be consistent with the abiding spirit of India, but framed to fit into a greater harmonised rhythm and plastic to the call of a more luminous future. If faith in ourselves and fidelity to the spirit of our culture are the first requisites of a continued and vigorous life, a recognition of greater possibilities is a condition not less indispensable. There cannot be a healthy and victorious survival if we make of the past a fetish instead of an inspiring impulse.

The spirit and ideals of our civilisation need no defence, for in their best parts and in their essence they were of eternal value. India's internal and individual seeking of them was earnest, powerful, effective. But the application in the collective life of society was subjected to serious reserves. Never sufficiently bold and thoroughgoing, it became more and more limited and halting when the lifeforce declined in her peoples. This defect, this gulf between ideal and collective practice, has pursued all human living and was not peculiar to India; but the dissonance became especially marked with the lapse of time and it put at last on our society a growing stamp of weakness and failure. There was a large effort in the beginning at some kind of synthesis between the inner ideal and the outer life; but a static regulation of society was its latter end. An underlying principle of spiritual idealism, an elusive unity and fixed helpful forms of mutuality remained always there, but also an increasing element of strict bondage and minute division and fissiparous complexity in the social mass. The great Vedantic ideals of freedom, unity and the godhead in man were left to the inner spiritual effort of individuals. The power of expansion and assimilation diminished and when powerful and aggressive forces broke in from outside, Islam, Europe, the later Hindu society was content with an imprisoned and static selfpreservation, a mere permission to live. The form of living became more and more narrow and it endured a continually restricted assertion of its ancient spirit. Duration, survival was achieved, but not in the end a really secure and vital duration, not a great, robust and victorious survival.

And now survival itself has become impossible without expansion. If we are to live at all, we must resume India's great interrupted endeavour; we must take up boldly and execute thoroughly in the individual and in the society, in the spiritual and in the mundane life, in philosophy and religion, in art and literature, in thought, in political and economic and social formulation the full and unlimited sense of her highest spirit and knowledge. And if we do that, we shall find that the best of what comes to us draped in occidental forms, is already implied in our own ancient wisdom and has there a greater spirit behind it, a profounder truth and selfknowledge and the capacity of a will to nobler and more ideal formations. Only we need to work out thoroughly in life what we have always known in the spirit. There and nowhere else lies the secret of the needed harmony between the essential meaning of our past culture and the environmental requirements of our future.

That view opens out a prospect beyond the battle of cultures which is the immediate dangerous aspect of the meeting of east and west. The Spirit in man has one aim before it in all mankind; but different continents or peoples approach it from different sides, with different formulations and in a differing spirit. Not recognising the underlying unity of the ultimate divine motive, they give battle to each other and claim that theirs alone is the way for mankind. The one real and perfect civilisation is the one in which they happen to be born, all the rest must perish or go under. But the real and perfect civilisation yet waits to be discovered; for the life of mankind is still nine tenths of barbarism to one tenth of culture. The European mind gives the first place to the principle of growth by struggle; it is by struggle that it arrives at some kind of concert. But this concert is itself hardly more than an organisation for growth by competition, aggression and farther battle. It is a peace that is constantly breaking, even within itself, into a fresh strife of principles, ideas, interests, races, classes. It is an organisation precarious at its base and in its centre because it is founded on halftruths that deteriorate into whole falsehoods; but it is still or has been till now vigorous in constant achievement and able to grow powerfully and to devour and assimilate. Indian culture proceeded on the principle of a concert that strove to find its base in a unity and reached out again towards some greater oneness. Its aim was a lasting organisation that would minimise or even eliminate the principle of struggle. But it ended by achieving peace and stable arrangement through exclusion, fragmentation and immobility of status; it drew a magic circle of safety and shut itself up in it for good. In the end it lost its force of aggression, weakened its power of assimilation and decayed within its barriers. A static and limited concert, not always enlarging itself, not plastic becomes in our human state of imperfection a prison or a sleeping chamber. Concert cannot be anything but imperfect and provisional in its form and can only preserve its vitality and fulfil its ultimate aim if it constantly adapts, expands, progresses. Its lesser unities must widen towards a broader and more comprehensive and above all a more real and spiritual oneness. In the larger statement of our culture and civilisation that we have now to achieve, a greater outward expression of spiritual and psychological oneness, but with a diversity which the mechanical method of Europe does not tolerate, will surely be one leading motive. A concert, a unity with the rest of mankind, in which we shall maintain our spiritual and our outer independence will be another line of our endeavour. But what now appears as a struggle may well be the first necessary step, before we can formulate that unity of mankind which the West sees only in idea, but cannot achieve because it does not possess its spirit. Therefore Europe labours to establish unity by accommodation of conflicting interests and the force of mechanical institutions; but so attempted, it will either not be founded at all or will be founded on sand. Meanwhile she wishes to blot out every other culture, as if hers were the only truth or all the truth of life and there were no such thing as truth of the spirit. India, the ancient possessor of the truth of the spirit, must resist that arrogant claim and aggression and affirm her own deeper truths in spite of heavy odds and against all comers. For in its preservation lies the only hope that mankind instead of marching to a new cataclysm and primitive beginning with a constant repetition of the old blind cycles will at last emerge into the light and accomplish the drive forward which will bring the terrestrial evolution to its next step of ascent in the progressive manifestation of the Spirit.

...The task of religion and spirituality is to mediate between God and man, between the Eternal and Infinite and this transient, yet persistent finite, between a luminous Truthconsciousness not expressed or not yet expressed here and the Mind's ignorance. But nothing is more difficult than to bring home the greatness and uplifting power of the spiritual consciousness to the natural man forming the vast majority of the race; for his mind and senses are turned outward towards the external calls of life and its objects and never inwards to the Truth which lies behind them. This external vision and attraction are the essence of the universal blinding force which is designated in Indian philosophy the ignorance. Ancient Indian spirituality recognised that man lives in the ignorance and has to be led through its imperfect indications to a highest inmost knowledge. Our life moves between two worlds, the depths upon depths of our inward being and the surface field of our outward nature. The majority of men put the whole emphasis of life on the outward and live very strongly in their surface consciousness and very little in the inward existence. Even the choice spirits raised from the grossness of the common vital and physical mould by the stress of thought and culture do not usually get farther than a strong dwelling on the things of the mind. The highest flight they reach and it is this that the west persistently mistakes for spirituality is a preference for living in the mind and emotions more than in the gross outward life or else an attempt to subject this rebellious life stuff to the law of intellectual truth or ethical reason and will or aesthetic beauty or of all three together. But spiritual knowledge perceives that there is a greater thing in us; our inmost self, our real being is not the intellect, not the aesthetic, ethical or thinking mind, but the divinity within, the Spirit, and these other things are only the instruments of the Spirit. A mere intellectual, ethical and aesthetic culture does not go back to the inmost truth of the spirit; it is still an ignorance, an incomplete, outward and superficial knowledge. To have made the discovery of our deepest being and hidden spiritual nature is the first necessity and to have erected the living of an inmost spiritual life into the aim of existence is the characteristic sign of a spiritual culture.

This endeavour takes in certain religions the form of a spiritual exclusiveness which revolts from the outward existence rather than seeks to transform it. The main tendency of the Christian discipline was not only to despise the physical and vital way of living, but to disparage and imprison the intellectual and distrust and discourage the aesthetic thirsts of our nature. It emphasised against them a limited spiritual emotionalism and its intense experiences as the one thing needful; the development of the ethical sense was the sole mental necessity, its translation into act the sole indispensable condition or result of the spiritual life. Indian spirituality reposed on too wide and manysided a culture to admit as its base this narrow movement; but on its more solitary summits, at least in its later period, it tended to a spiritual exclusiveness loftier in vision, but even more imperative and excessive. A spirituality of this intolerant high pointed kind, to whatever elevation it may rise, however it may help to purify life or lead to a certain kind of individual salvation, cannot be a complete thing. For its exclusiveness imposes on it a certain impotence to deal effectively with the problems of human existence; it cannot lead it to its integral perfection or combine its highest heights with its broadest broadness. A wider spiritual culture must recognise that the Spirit is not only the highest and inmost thing, but all is manifestation and creation of the Spirit. It must have a wider outlook, a more embracing range of applicability and, even, a more aspiring and ambitious aim of its endeavour. Its aim must be not only to raise to inaccessible heights the few elect, but to draw all men and all life and the whole human being upward, to spiritualise life and in the end to divinise human nature. Not only must it be able to lay hold on his deepest individual being but to inspire too his communal existence. It must turn by a spiritual change all the members of his ignorance into members of the knowledge; it must transmute all the instruments of the human into instruments of a divine living. The total movement of Indian spirituality is towards this aim; in spite of all the difficulties, imperfections and fluctuations of its evolution, it had this character. But like other cultures it was not at all times and in all its parts and movements consciously aware of its own total significance. This large sense sometimes emerged into something like a conscious synthetic clarity, but was more often kept in the depths and on the surface dispersed in a multitude of subordinate and special standpoints. Still, it is only by an intelligence of the total drift that its manifold sides and rich variations of effort and teaching and discipline can receive their full reconciling unity and be understood in the light of its own most intrinsic purpose.

Now the spirit of Indian religion and spiritual culture has been persistently and immovably the same throughout the long time of its vigour, but its form has undergone remarkable changes. Yet if we look into them from the right centre it will be apparent that these changes are the results of a logical and inevitable evolution inherent in the very process of man's growth towards the heights. In its earliest form, its first vedic system, it took its outward foundation on the mind of the physical man whose natural faith is in things physical, in the sensible and visible objects, presences, representations and the external pursuits and aims of this material world, The means, symbols, rites, figures, by which it sought to mediate between the spirit and the normal human mentality were drawn from these most external physical things. Man's first and primitive idea of the Divine can only come through his vision of external Nature and the sense of a superior Power or Powers concealed behind her phenomena, veiled in the heaven and earth, father and mother of our being, in the sun and moon and stars, its lights and regulators, in dawn and day and night and rain and wind and storm, the oceans and the rivers and the forests, all the circumstances and forces of her scene of action, all that vast and mysterious surrounding life of which we are a part and in which the natural heart and mind of the human creature feel instinctively through whatever bright or dark or confused figures that there is here some divine Multitude or else mighty Infinite, one, manifold and mysterious, which takes these forms and manifests itself in these motions. The Vedic religion took this natural sense and feeling of the physical man; it used the conceptions to which they gave birth, and it sought to lead him through them to the psychic and spiritual truths of his own being and the being of the cosmos. It recognised that he was right when he saw behind the manifestations of Nature great living powers and godheads, even though he knew not their inner truth, and right too in offering to them worship and propitiation and atonement. For that inevitably must be the initial way in which his active physical, vital and mental nature is allowed to approach the Godhead, He approaches it through its visible outward manifestations as something greater than his own natural self, something single or multiple that guides, sustains and directs his life, and he calls to it for help and support in the desires and difficulties and distresses and struggles of his human existence. The Vedic religion accepted also the form in which early man everywhere expressed his sense of the relation between himself and the godheads of Nature; it adopted as its central symbol the act and ritual of a physical sacrifice. However crude the notions attached to it, this idea of the necessity of sacrifice did express obscurely a first law of being. For it was founded on that secret of constant interchange between the individual and the universal powers of the cosmos which covertly supports all the process of life and develops the action of Nature.

But even in its external or exoteric side the Vedic religion did not limit itself to this acceptance and regulation of the first religious notions of the natural physical mind of man. The Vedic Rishis gave a psychic function to the godheads worshipped by the people; they spoke to them of a higher Truth, Right, Law of which the gods were the guardians, of the necessity of a truer knowledge and a larger inner living according to this Truth and Right and of a home of Immortality to which the soul of man could ascend by the power of Truth and of right doing. The people no doubt took these ideas in their most external sense; but they were trained by them to develop their ethical nature, to turn towards some initial development of their psychic being, to conceive the idea of a knowledge and truth other than that of the physical life and to admit even a first conception of some greater spiritual Reality which was the ultimate object of human worship or aspiration. This religious and moral force was the highest reach of the external cult and the most that could be understood or followed by the mass of the people.

The deeper truth of these things was reserved for the initiates, for those who were ready to understand and practise the inner sense, the esoteric meaning hidden in the Vedic scripture. For the Veda is full of words which, as the Rishis themselves express it, are secret words that give their inner meaning only to the seer, kavaye nivacana ninya vacamsi. This is a feature of the ancient sacred hymns which grew obscure to later ages; it became a dead tradition and has been entirely ignored by modern scholarship in its laborious attempt to read the hieroglyph of the Vedic symbols. Yet its recognition is essential to a right understanding of almost all the ancient religions; for mostly they started on their upward curve through an esoteric element of which the key was not given to all. In all or most there was a surface cult for the common physical man who was held yet unfit for the psychic and spiritual life and an inner secret of the Mysteries carefully disguised by symbols whose sense was opened only to the initiates. This was the origin of the later distinction between the Shudra, the undeveloped physical minded man, and the twice born, those who were capable of entering into the second birth by initiation and to whom alone the Vedic education could be given without danger. This too actuated the later prohibition of any reading or teaching of the Veda by the Shudra. It was this inner meaning, it was the higher psychic and spiritual truths concealed by the outer sense, that gave to these hymns the name by which they are still known, the Veda, the Book of Knowledge. Only by penetrating into the esoteric sense of this worship can we understand the full flowering of the Vedic religion in the Upanishads and in the later evolution of the Indian spiritual search and experience. For it is all there in its luminous seed, preshadowed or even prefigured in the verses of the early seers. The persistent notion, which through every change, is ascribed the foundation of all our culture to the Rishis, whatever its fabulous forms and mythical ascriptions, contains a real truth and veils a sound historical tradition. It reflects the fact of a true initiation and an unbroken continuity between this great primitive past and the more developed hardly greater spiritual development of our historical culture.

This inner Vedic religion started with an extension of the psychic significance of the godheads in the Cosmos. Its primary notion was that of a hierarchy of the worlds, an ascending stair of the planes of being in the universe. It saw a mounting scale of the worlds corresponding to a similar mounting scale of planes or degrees or levels of consciousness in the nature of man. The Truth, Right and Law sustain and govern all these levels of Nature; one in essence, it takes in them different but cognate forms. There is, for instance, a series of the outer physical light, another higher and inner light which is the vehicle of the mental, vital and psychic consciousness and the highest innermost light of the spiritual illumination. Surya, the Sun God, was the lord of the physical Sun; but he is, at the same time, to the Vedic seerpoet, the giver of the rays of knowledge which illumine the mind and he is also the soul and energy and body of the spiritual illumination. And in all these powers, he is a luminous form of the one and infinite Godhead, All the Vedic godheads have this outer, inner and the innermost function, their known and their secret Names. All are in their external character the powers of the physical Nature; all have in their inner meaning a psychic function and the psychological ascriptions; all are various powers of one highest Reality, ekam sat, the one infinite Existence. This hardly knowable Supreme is often called in the Veda "That Truth" or "That One", tat satyam, tad ekam. This complex character of the Vedic godheads assumes forms which have been wholly misunderstood by those who ascribe to them only their outward physical significance. Each of these gods is in himself a complete and separate cosmic personality of the one existence and in their combination of powers they form the complete universal power, the cosmic whole, vaisvadevyam. Each again, apart from his special function, is one godhead with the others; each holds in himself the universal divinity, each god is all the other gods. This is the aspect of the Vedic teaching and worship to which a European scholar, mistaking entirely its significance because he read it in the dim and poor light of European religious experience, has given the sounding misnomer, henotheism. Beyond, in the triple Infinite, these godheads put on their highest nature and are names of the one nameless Ineffable.

But the greatest power of the Vedic teaching, that which made it the source of all later Indian philosophies, religions, systems of Yoga, lay in its application to the inner life of man. Man lives in the physical cosmos subject to death and the "much falsehood" of the mortal existence. To rise beyond this death, to become one of the immortals, he has to turn from the falsehood to the Truth; he has to turn to the Light and to battle with and to conquer the powers of the Darkness. This he does by communion with the divine Powers and their aid; the way to call down this aid was the secret of the Vedic mystics. The symbols of the outer sacrifice are given for this purpose in the manner of the Mysteries all over the world an inner meaning; they represent a calling of the gods into the human being, a connecting sacrifice, an intimate interchange, a mutual aid, a communion. There is a building of the powers of the godheads within man and a formation in him of the universality of the divine nature. For the gods are the guardians and increasers of the Truth, the powers of the Immortal, the sons of the infinite Mother; the way to immortality is the upward way of the gods, the way of the Truth, a journey, an ascent by which there is a growth into the law of the Truth, rtasya panthah. Man arrives at immortality by breaking beyond the limitations not only of his physical self, but of his mental and his ordinary psychic nature into the highest plane and supreme ether of the Truth: for there is the foundation of immortality and the native seat of the triple Infinite. On these ideas the Vedic sages built up a profound psychological and psychic discipline which led beyond itself to a highest spirituality and contained the nucleus of later Indian Yoga. Already we find in their seed, though not in their full expansion, the most characteristic ideas of Indian spirituality. There is the one existence, ekam sat, supracosmic beyond the individual and the universe. There is the one God who presents to us the many forms, names, powers, personalities of his Godhead. There is the distinction between the knowledge and the ignorance, the greater truth of an immortal life opposed to the much falsehood or mixed truth and falsehood of mortal existence. There is the discipline of an inward growth of man from the physical through the psychic to the spiritual existence. There is the conquest of death, the secret of immortality, the perception of a realisable divinity of the human spirit. In an age to which in the insolence of our external knowledge we are accustomed to look back as the childhood of humanity or at best a period of vigorous barbarism, this was the inspired and intuitive psychic and spiritual teaching by which the ancient human fathers, purve pitarah manusydh, founded a great and profound civilisation in India.

This high beginning was secured in its results by a larger sublime efflorescence. The Upanishads have always been recognised in India as the crown and end of Veda. that is indicated in their general name, Vedanta. And they are in fact a large crowning outcome of the Vedic discipline and experience. The time in which the Vedantic truth was wholly seen and the Upanishads took shape, was, as we can discern from such records as the Chhandogya and Brihadaranyaka, an epoch of immense and strenuous seeking, an intense and ardent seed time of the Spirit. In the stress of that seeking the truths held by the initiates but kept back from ordinary men broke their barriers, swept through the higher mind of the nation and fertilised the soil of Indian culture for a constant and ever increasing growth of spiritual consciousness and spiritual experience. This turn was not as yet universal; it was chiefly men of the higher classes, Kshatriyas and Brahmins trained in the Vedic system of education, no longer content with an external truth and the works of the outer sacrifice, who began everywhere to seek for the highest word of revealing experience from the sages who possessed the knowledge of the One. But we find too among those who attained to the knowledge and became great teachers men of inferior or doubtful birth like Janashruti, the wealthy Shudra, or Satyakama Jabali, son of a servant girl who knew not who was his father. The work that was done in this period became the firm bedrock of Indian spirituality in later ages and from it gush still the life giving waters of a perennial and never failing inspiration. This period, this activity, this grand achievement created the whole difference between the evolution of Indian civilisation and the quite different curve of other cultures.

For a time had come when the original Vedic symbols must lose their significance and pass into an obscurity that became impenetrable, as did the inner teaching of the mysteries in other countries. The old poise of culture between two extremes with a bridge of religious cult and symbolism to unite them, the crude or half trained naturalness of the outer physical man on one side of the line, and on the other an inner and secret psychic and spiritual life for the initiates could no longer suffice as the basis of our spiritual progress. The human race in its cycle of civilisation needed a large lined advance; it called for a more and more generalised intellectual, ethical and aesthetic evolution to help it to grow into the light. This turn had to come in India as in other lands. But the danger was that the greater spiritual truth already gained might be lost in the lesser confident half light of the acute but unillumined intellect or stifled within the narrow limits of the selfsufficient logical reason. That was what actually happened in the West, Greece leading the way. The old knowledge was prolonged in a less inspired, less dynamic and more intellectual form by the Pythagoreans, by the Stoics, by Plato and the Neo-Platonists; hut still in spite of them and in spite of the only half illumined spiritual wave which swept over Europe from Asia in an ill understood Christianity, the whole real trend of Western civilisation has been intellectual, rational, secular and even materialistic, and it keeps this character to the present day. Its general aim has been a strong or a fine culture of the vital and physical man by the power of an intellectualised ethics, aesthesis and reason, not the leading up of our lower members into the supreme light and power of the spirit. The ancient spiritual knowledge and the spiritual tendency it had created were saved in India from this collapse by the immense effort of the age of the Upanishads. The Vedantic seers renewed the Vedic truth by extricating it from its cryptic symbols and casting it into a highest and most direct and powerful language of intuition and inner experience. It was not the language of the intellect, but still it wore a form which the intellect could take hold of, translate into its own more abstract terms and convert into a starting point for an ever widening and deepening philosophic speculation and the reason's long search after a Truth original, supreme and ultimate. There was in India as in the West a great up building of a high, wide and complex intellectual, aesthetic, ethical and social culture. But left in Europe to its own resources, combated rather than helped by obscure religious emotion and dogma, here it was guided, uplifted and more and more penetrated and suffused by a great saving power of spirituality and a vast stimulating and tolerant light of wisdom from a highest ether of knowledge.

The second, or post-Vedic age of Indian civilisation was distinguished by the rise of the great philosophies, by a copious, vivid, many thoughted, manysided epic literature, by the beginnings of art and science, by the evolution of a vigorous and complex society, by the formation of large kingdoms and empires, by manifold formative activities of all kinds and great systems of living and thinking. Here as elsewhere, in Greece, Rome, Persia, China, this was the age of a high outburst of the intelligence working upon life and the things of the mind to discover their reason and their right way and bring out a broad and noble fullness of human existence. But in India this effort never lost sight of the spiritual motive, never missed the touch of the religious sense. It was a birth time and youth of the seeking intellect and, as in Greece, philosophy was the main instrument by which it laboured to solve the problems of life and the world. Science too developed, but it came second only as an auxiliary power. It was through profound and subtle philosophies that the intellect of India attempted to analyse by the reason and logical faculty what had formerly been approached with a much more living force through intuition and the soul's experience. But the philosophic mind started from the data these mightier powers had discovered and was faithful to its parent Light; it went back always in one form or another to the profound truths of the Upanishads which kept their place as the highest authority in these matters. There was a constant admission that spiritual experience is a greater thing and its light a truer if more incalculable guide than the clarities of the reasoning intelligence. The same governing force kept its hold on all the other activities of the Indian mind and Indian life. The epic literature is full almost to excess of a strong and free intellectual and ethical thinking; there is an incessant criticism of life by the intelligence and the ethical reason, an arresting curiosity and desire to fix the norm of truth in all possible fields. But in the background and coming constantly to the front there is too a constant religious sense and an implicit or avowed assent to the spiritual truths which remained the unshakable basis of the culture. These truths suffused with their higher light secular thought and action or stood above to remind them that they were only steps towards a goal. Art in India, contrary to a common idea, dwelt much upon life; but still its highest achievement was always in the field of the interpretation of the religiophilosophical mind and its whole tone was coloured by a suggestion of the spiritual and the infinite. Indian society developed with an unsurpassed organising ability, stable effectiveness, practical insight its communal coordination of the mundane life of interest and desire, kama, artha it governed always its action by a reference at every point to the moral and religious law, the Dharma: but it never lost sight of spiritual liberation as our highest point and the ultimate aim of the effort of Life. In later times when there was a still stronger secular tendency of intellectual culture, there Came in an immense development of the mundane intelligence, an opulent political and social evolution, an emphatic stressing of aesthetic, sensuous and hedonistic experience. But this effort too always strove to keep itself within the ancient frame and not to lose the special stamp of the Indian cultural idea. The enlarged secular turn was compensated by a deepening of the intensities of psychoreligious experience. New religious or mystic forms and disciplines attempted to seize not only the soul and the intellect, but the emotions, the senses, the vital and the aesthetic nature of man and turn them into stuff of the spiritual life. And every excess of emphasis on the splendour and richness and power and pleasures of life had its recoil and was balanced by a corresponding potent stress on spiritual asceticism as the higher way. The two trends, on one side an extreme of the richness of life experience, on the other an extreme and pure rigorous intensity of the spiritual life, accompanied each other; their interaction, whatever loss there might be of the earlier deep harmony and large synthesis, yet by their double pull preserved something still of the balance of Indian culture.

Indian religion followed this line of evolution and kept its in-ner continuity with its Vedic and Vedantic origins; but it changed entirely its mental contents and colour and its outward basis. It did not effectuate this change through any protestant revolt or revolution or with any idea of an iconoclastic reformation. A continuous development of its organic life took place, a natural transformation brought out latent motives or else gave to already established motive ideas a more predominant place or effective form. At one time indeed it seemed as if a discontinuity and a sharp new beginning were needed and would take place. Buddhism seemed to reject all spiritual continuity with the Vedic religion. But this was after all less in reality than in appearance. The Buddhist ideal of Nirvana was no more than a sharply negative and exclusive statement of the highest Vedantic spiritual experience. The ethical system of the eightfold path taken as the way to release was an austere sublimation of the Vedic notion of the Right, Truth and Law followed as the way to immortality, rtasya panthah. The strongest note of Mahayana Buddhism, its stress on universal compassion and fellow feeling, was an ethical application of the spiritual unity which is the essential idea of Vedanta. The most characteristic tenets of the new discipline, Nirvana and Karma, could have been supported from the utterances of the Brahmanas and Upanishads. Buddhism could easily have claimed for itself a Vedic origin and the claim would have been no less valid than the Vedic ascription of the Sankhya philosophy and discipline with which it had some points of intimate alliance. But what hurt Buddhism and determined in the end its rejection, was not its denial of a Vedic origin or authority, but the exclusive trenchancy of its intellectual, ethical and spiritual positions. A result of an intense stress of the union of logical reason with the spiritualised mind for it was by an intense spiritual search supported on a clear and hard rational thinking that it was born as a separate religion, its trenchant affirmations and still more exclusive negations could not be made sufficiently compatible with the native flexibility, manysided susceptibility and rich synthetic turn of the Indian religious consciousness; it was a high creed but not plastic enough to hold the heart of the people. Indian religion absorbed all that it could of Buddhism, but rejected its exclusive positions and preserved the full line of its own continuity, casting back to the ancient Vedanta.

This lasting line of change moved forward not by any destruction of principle, but by a gradual fading out of the prominent Vedic forms and the substitution of others. There was a transformation of symbol and ritual and ceremony or a substitution of new kindred figures, an emergence of things that are only hints in the original system, a development of novel idea forms from the seed of the original thinking. And especially there was a farther widening and fathoming of psychic and spiritual experience. The Vedic gods rapidly lost their deep original significance. At first they kept their hold by their outer cosmic sense hut were overshadowed by the great Trinity, Brahma-Vishnu-Shiva, and afterwards faded altogether. A new pantheon appeared which in its outward symbolic aspects expressed a deeper truth and larger range of religious experience, an intenser feeling, a vaster idea. The Vedic sacrifice persisted only in broken and lessening fragments. The house of Fire was replaced by the temple; the karmic ritual of sacrifice was transformed into the devotional temple ritual; the vague and shifting mental images of the Vedic gods figured in the mantras yielded to more precise conceptual forms of the two great deities, Vishnu and Shiva, and of their Shaktis and their offshoots. These new concepts stabilised in physical images which were made the basis both for internal adoration and for the external worship which replaced sacrifice. The psychic and spiritual mystic endeavour which was the inner sense of the Vedic hymns, disappeared into the less intensely luminous but more wide and rich and complex psychospiritual inner life of Puranic and Tantric religion and Yoga.

The Purano-Tantric stage of the religion was once decried by European critics and Indian reformers as a base and ignorant degradation of an earlier and purer religion. It was rather an effort, successful in a great measure, to open the general mind of the people to a higher and deeper range of inner truth and experience and feeling. Much of the adverse criticism once heard proceeded from a total ignorance of the sense and intention of this worship. Much of this criticism has been uselessly concentrated on sidepaths and aberrations which could hardly be avoided in this immensely audacious experimental widening of the basis of the culture. For there was a catholic attempt to draw towards the spiritual truth minds of all qualities and people of all classes. Much was lost of the profound psychic knowledge of the Vedic seers, but much also of new knowledge was developed," untrodden ways were opened and a hundred gates discovered into the Infinite. If we try to see the essential sense and aim of this development and the intrinsic value of its forms and means and symbols, we shall find that this evolution followed upon the early Vedic form very much for the same reason as Catholic Christianity replaced the mysteries and sacrifices of the early Pagan religions. For in both cases the outward basis of the early religion spoke to the outward physical mind of the people and took that as the starting point of its appeal. But the new evolution tried to awaken a more inner mind even in the common man, to lay hold on his inner vital and emotional nature, to support all by an awakening of the soul and to lead him through these things towards a highest spiritual truth. It attempted in fact to bring the mass into the temple of the spirit rather than leave them in the outer precincts. The outward physical sense was satisfied through its aesthetic turn by a picturesque temple worship, by numerous ceremonies, by the use of physical images; but these were given a psychoemotional sense and direction that was open to the heart and imagination of the ordinary man and not reserved for the deeper sight of the elect or the strenuous tapasya of the initiates. The secret initiation remained but was now a condition for the passage from the surface psychoemotional and religious to a profounder psychicspiritual truth and experience.

Nothing essential was touched in its core by this new orientation; but the instruments, atmosphere, field of religious experience underwent a considerable change. The Vedic god-heads were to the mass of their worshippers divine powers who presided over the workings of the outward life of the physical cosmos; the Puranic Trinity had even for the multitude a predominant psychoreligious and spiritual significance. Its more external significances, for instance the functions of cosmic creation, preservation and destruction, were only a dependent fringe of these profundities that alone touched the heart of its mystery. The central spiritual truth remained in both systems the same, the truth of the One in many aspects. The Trinity is a triple form of the one supreme Godhead and Brahman; the Shaktisare energies of the one Energy of the highest divine Being. But this greatest religious truth was no longer reserved for the initiated few; it was now more and more brought powerfully, widely and intensely home to the general mind and feeling of the people. Even the socalled henotheism of the Vedic idea was prolonged and heightened in the larger and simpler worship of Vishnu or Shiva as the one universal and highest Godhead of whom all others are living forms and powers. The idea of the Divinity in man was popularised to an extraordinary extent, not only the occasional manifestation of the Divine in humanity which founded the worship of the Avataras, but the Presence discoverable in the heart of every creature. The systems of Yoga developed themselves on the same common basis. All led or hoped to lead through many kinds of psychophysical, inner vital, inner mental and psychospiritual methods to the common aim of all Indian spirituality, a greater consciousness and a more or less complete union with the One and Divine or else an immergence of the individual soul in the Absolute. The Purano-Tantric system was a wide, assured and manysided endeavour, unparalleled in its power, insight, amplitude, to provide the race with a basis of generalised psychoreligious experience from which man could rise through knowledge, works or love or through any other fundamental power of his nature to some established supreme experience and highest absolute status.

This great effort and achievement which covered all the time between the Vedic age and the decline of Buddhism, was still not the last possibility of religious evolution open to Indian culture. The Vedic training of the physically minded man made the development possible. But in its turn this raising of the basis of religion to the inner mind and life and psychic nature, this training and bringing out of the psychic man ought to make possible a still larger development and support a greater spiritual movement as the leading power of life. The first stage makes possible the preparation of the natural external man for spirituality; the second takes up his outward life into a deeper mental and psychical living and brings him more directly into contact with the spirit and divinity within him; the third should render him capable of taking up his whole mental, psychical, physical living into a first beginning at least of a generalised spiritual life. This endeavour has manifested itself in the evolution of Indian spirituality and is the significance of the latest philosophies, the great spiritual movements of the saints and bhaktas and an increasing resort to the various paths of Yoga. But unhappily it synchronised with a decline of Indian culture and an increasing collapse of its general power and knowledge, and in these surroundings it could not bear its natural fruit; but at the same time it has done much to prepare such a possibility in the future. If Indian culture is to survive and keep its spiritual basis and innate character, it is in this direction, and not in a mere revival or prolongation of the Puranic system, that its evolution must turn, rising so towards the fulfilment of that which the Vedic seers saw as the aim of man and his life thousands of years ago and the Vedantic sages cast into the clear and immortal forms of their luminous revelation. Even the psychice motional part of man's nature is not the inmost door to religious feeling, nor is his inner mind the highest witness to spiritual experience.

There is behind the first the inmost soul of man, in that deepest secret heart, hrdaye guhayam, in which the ancient seers saw the very tabernacle of the indwelling Godhead and there is above the second a luminous highest mind directly open to a truth of the Spirit to which man's normal nature has as yet only an occasional and momentary access. Religious evolution, spiritual experience can find their true native road only when they open to these hidden powers and make them their support for a lasting change, a divinisation of human life and nature. An effort of this kind was the very force behind the most luminous and vivid of the later movements of India's vast religious cycle. It is the secret of the most powerful forms of Vaishnavism and Tantra and Yoga. The labour of ascent from our half animal human nature into the fresh purity of the spiritual consciousness needed to be followed and supplemented by a descent of the light and force of the spirit into man's members and the attempt to transform human into divine nature.

But it could not find its complete way or its fruit because it synchronised with a decline of the life force in India and a lowering of power and knowledge in her general civilisation and culture. Nevertheless here lies the destined force of her survival and renewal, this is the dynamic meaning of her future. A widest and highest spiritualising of life on earth is the last vision of all that vast and unexampled seeking and experiment in a thousand ways of the soul's outermost and innermost experience which is the unique character of her past; this in the end is the mission for which she was born and the meaning of her existence.

...Indian culture recognises the spirit as the truth of our being and our life as a growth and evolution of the spirit. It sees the Eternal, the Infinite, the Supreme, the All; it sees this as the secret highest Self of all, this is what it calls God, the Permanent, the Real, and it sees man as a soul and power of this being of God in Nature. The progressive growth of the finite consciousness of man towards this Self, towards God, towards the universal, the eternal, the infinite, in a word his growth into spiritual con-sciousness, by the development of his ordinary ignorant natural being into an illumined divine nature, this is for Indian thinking the significance of life and the aim of human existence. To this deeper and more spiritual idea of Nature and of existence a great deal of what is strongest and most potential of fruitful consequences in recent European thinking already turns with a growing impetus. This turn may be a relapse to "barbarism" or it may be the high natural outcome of her own increasing and ripened culture; that is a question for Europe to decide. But always to India this ideal inspiration or rather this spiritual vision of Self, God, Spirit, this nearness to a cosmic consciousness, a cosmic sense and feeling, a cosmic idea, will, love, delight into which we can release the limited, ignorant, suffering ego, this drive towards the transcendental, eternal and infinite, and the moulding of man into a conscious soul and power of that greater Existence have been the engrossing motive of her philosophy, the sustaining force of her religion, the fundamental idea of her civilisation and culture.

I have suggested that the formal turn, the rhythmic lines of effort of this culture must be regarded as having passed through two complete external stages; while a third has taken its initial steps and is the destiny of her future. The early Vedic was the first stage: then religion took its outward formal stand on the natural approach of the physical mind of man to the Godhead in the universe, but the initiates guarded the sacrificial fire of a greater spiritual truth behind the form. The Purano-Tantric was the second stage: then religion took its outward formal stand on the first deeper approaches of man's inner mind and life to the Divine in the universe, but a greater initiation opened the way to a far more intimate truth and pushed towards an inner living of the spiritual life in all its profundity and in all the infinite possibilities of an uttermost sublime experience. There has been long in preparation a third stage which belongs to the future. Its inspiring idea has been often cast out in limited or large, veiled and quiet or bold and striking spiritual movements and potent new disciplines and religions, but it has not yet been successful in finding its way or imposing new lines on human life. The circumstances were adverse, the hour not yet come. This greatest movement of the Indian spiritual mind has a double impulse. Its will is to call the community of men and all men each according to his power to live in the greatest light of all and found their whole life on some fully revealed power and grand uplifting truth of the Spirit. But it has had too at times a highest vision which sees the possibility not only of an ascent towards the Eternal descent of the Divine Consciousness and a change of human into divine nature. A perception of the divinity hidden in man has been its crowning force. This is a turn that cannot be rightly understood in the ideas or language of the European religious reformer or his imitators. It is not what the purist of the reason or the purist of the spirit imagines it to be and by that too hasty imagination falls short in his endeavour. Its index vision is pointed to a truth that exceeds the human mind and, if at all realised in his members, would turn human life into a divine superlife. And not until this third largest sweep of the spiritual evolution has come into its own, can Indian civilisation be said to have discharged its mission, to have spoken its last word and be functus office, crowned and complete in its office of mediation between the life of man and the spirit.

The past dealings of Indian religion with life must be judged according to the stages of its progress; each age of its movement must be considered on its own basis. But throughout it consistently held to two perceptions that showed great practical wisdom and a fine spiritual tact. First, it saw that the approach to the spirit cannot be sudden, simple and immediate for all individuals or for the community of men; it must come ordinarily or at least at first through a gradual culture, training, progress. There must be an enlarging of the natural life accompanied by an uplifting of all its motives; a growing hold upon it of the higher rational, psychic and ethical powers must prepare and lead it towards a higher spiritual law. But the Indian religious mind saw too at the same time that if its greater aim was to be fruitful and the character of its culture imperative, there must be throughout and at every moment some kind of insistence on the spiritual motive. And for the mass of men this means always some kind of religious influence. That pervasive insistence was necessary in order that from the beginning some power of the universal inner truth, some ray from the real reality of our existence might cast its light or at least its sensible if subtle influence on the natural life of man. Human life must be induced to flower, naturally in a way, but at the same time with a wise nurturing and cultivation into its own profounder spiritual significance. Indian culture has worked by two coordinated, mutually stimulating and always interblended operations of which these perceptions are the principle. First, it has laboured to lead upward and enlarge the life of the individual in the community through a natural series of life stages till it was ready for the spiritual levels. But also it has striven to keep that highest aim before the mind at every Stage and throw its influence on each circumstance and action both of man's inner and his outer existence.

In the plan of its first aim it came nearer to the highest ancient culture of mankind in other regions, but in a type and with a motive all its own. The frame of its system was constituted by a triple quartette. Its first circle was the synthesis and gradation of the fourfold object of life, vital desire and hedonistic enjoyment, personal and communal interest, moral right and law, and spiritual liberation. Its second circle was the fourfold order of society, carefully graded and equipped with its fixed economic functions and its deeper cultural, ethical and spiritual significances. Its third, the most original and indeed unique of its englobing lifepatterns, was the fourfold scale of the successive stages of life, student, householder, forest recluse and free supersocial man. This frame, these lines of a large and noble lifetraining subsisted in their purity, their grand natural balance of austerity and accommodation, their fine effectiveness during the later Vedic and heroic age of the civilisation: afterwards they crumbled slowly or lost their completeness and order. But the tradition, the idea with some large effect of its force and some figure of its lines endured throughout the whole period of cultural vigour. However deflected it might have been from its true form and spirit, however mutilated and complicated for the worse, there was always left some presence of its inspiration and power. Only in the decline do we get the slow collapse, the degraded and confused mass of conventions which still labours to represent the ancient and noble Aryan system, but in spite of relics of glamour and beauty, in spite of survivals of spiritual suggestion and in spite of a residue of the old high training, is little better than a detritus or a mass of confused relics. Still even in this degradation enough of the original virtue has re-mained to ensure a remarkable remnant of the ancient beauty, attractiveness and power of survival.

But the turn given to the other and more direct spiritual operation of this culture is of a still greater importance. For it is that which, always surviving, has coloured permanently the Indian mind and life. It has remained the same behind every change of forms and throughout all the ages of the civilisation it has renewed its effectiveness and held its field. This second side of the cultural effort took the form of an endeavour to cast the whole of life into a religious mould; it multiplied means and devices which by their insistent suggestion and opportunity and their mass of effect would help to stamp a Godward tendency on the entire existence. Indian culture was founded on a religious conception of life and both the individual and the community drank in at every moment its influence. It was stamped on them by the training and turn of the education; the entire life atmosphere, all the social surroundings were suffused with it; it breathed its power through the whole original form and hieratic character of the culture. Always was felt the near idea of the spiritual existence and its supremacy as the ideal, highest over all others; everywhere there was the pervading pressure of the notion of the universe as a manifestation of divine Powers and a movement full of the presence of the Divine. Man himself was not a mere reasoning animal, but a soul in constant relation with God and with the divine cosmic powers. The soul's continued existence was a cyclic or upward progress from birth to birth; human life was the summit of an evolution which terminated in the conscious Spirit, every stage of that life a step in a pilgrimage. Every single action of man had its importance of fruit whether in future lives or in the worlds beyond the material existence.

But the Indian religion was not content with the general pressure of these conceptions, the training, the atmosphere and the stamp on the culture. Its persistent effort was to impress the mind at every moment and each particular area with the religious influence. And to do this more effectively by a living and practical adaptation, not asking from anyone what was too much or too little for him it took as a guiding idea its perception of the varying natural capacities of man, adhikara. It provided, in its system, the means by which each man, high or low, wise or ignorant, exceptional or average might feel, in the way suitable to his nature and evolutionary stage, the call, the pressure and the influence. Avoiding the error of the religions that impose a single dogmatic and inflexible rule on every man regardless of the possibilities of his nature, it tried rather to draw him gently upwards and help him to grow steadily in religious and spiritual experience. Every part of human nature, every characteristic turn of its action was given a place in the system; each was, suitably, surrounded with the spiritual idea and a religious influence, each provided with steps by which it might rise towards its own spiritual possibility and significance. The highest spiritual meaning of life was set on the summits of each evolving power of the human nature. The intelligence was called to a supreme knowledge, the dynamic active and creative powers pointed to openness and unity with an infinite and universal Will, the heart and sense put in contact with a divine love, joy and beauty. But this highest meaning was also put everywhere indicatively or in symbols behind the whole system of living, even its details, so that its impression might fall in whatever degree on the life, increase in pervasion and in the end, take up the entire control. This was the aim and, if we consider the imperfections of our nature and the difficulty of the endeavour, we can say that it achieved an unusual measure of success. It has been said with some truth, that for an Indian the whole of life is a religion. True of the ideal of Indian life, it is true to a certain degree and in a certain sense in its fact and practice. No step could be taken in the Indian's inner or outer life without his being reminded of a spiritual existence. Everywhere he felt the closeness or at least saw the sign of something beyond his natural life, beyond the moment in time, beyond his individual ego, something other than the needs and interests of his vital and physical nature. That insistence gave its tone and turn to his thought and action and feeling; it produced that subtle sensitivity to the spiritual appeal, a greater readiness to turn to the spiritual effort which are even now the distinguishing marks of the Indian temperament. It is that readiness, that sensitivity which justifies us when we speak of the characteristic spirituality of the Indian people.

The ancient idea of the adhikara has to be taken into a careful account if we want to understand the peculiar character of the Indian religion. In many religious systems, we find a highpitched spiritual call and a difficult and rigid ethical standard far beyond the possibilities of man's partially evolved, defective and imperfect nature. This standard, this call is announced as if imperative on all; but it is evident that only a few can give an adequate response. There is presented to our view for all our picture of life the sharp division of two extremes; the saint and the worldling, the religious and the irreligious, the good and the bad, the pious and the impious, the souls accepted and the souls rejected, the sheep and the goats, the saved and the damned, the believer and the infidel. Between these two extremes is chaos, a tug of war, an uncertain balance. This crude classification is the foundation of the Christian system of an eternal heaven and hell; at best, the Catholic religion, humanely, interposes a precarious "chance hung" between that happy and this dread alternative, the chance of a painful purgatory for more than nine-tenths of the human race. The Indian religion set up on its summits a still more highpitched spiritual call, a standard of conduct still more perfect and absolute; but it did not go about its work with this summarised and unreflecting ignorance. All beings are, to the Indian mind, portions of the Divine, evolving souls, and can be sure of an eventual salvation and release into the spirit. All must feel, as the good in them grows or, more truly, the godhead in them finds itself and becomes conscious, the ultimate touch and call of their highest self and through that call, the attraction to the Eternal and Divine. But, actually in life, there are infinite differences between man and man; some are more inwardly

universal compassion and benevolence calm and sweet in the perfect purity of the spirit, the upsurge of the psychical being into the spiritual unity or the spiritual ecstasy, these divinest things were the heritage of the human being ready for divinity and their way and call were the supreme significances of Indian religion and Yoga. He reached by them the fruits of his perfect spiritual evolution, an identity with the Self and Spirit, a dwelling in or with God, the divine law of his being, a spiritual universality, communion, transcendence.

But distinctions are lines that can always be overpassed in the infinite complexity of man's nature and there was no sharp and unbridgeable division, only a gradation, since the actuality or potentiality of the three powers coexist in all men. Both the middle and the highest significances were near and present and pervaded the whole system, and the approaches to the highest status were not absolutely denied to any man, in spite of certain prohibitions: but these prohibitions broke down in practice or left a way of escape to the man who felt the call; the call itself was a sign of election. He had only to find the way and the guide. But even in the direct approach the principle of adhikara, differing capacity and varying nature, svabhava, was recognised in subtle ways, which it would be beyond my present purpose to enumerate. One may note as an example the significant Indian idea of the istadevata, the special name, form, idea of the Divinity which each man may choose for worship and communion and follow after according to the attraction in his nature and his capacity of spiritual intelligence. And each of the forms has its outer initial associations and suggestions for the worshipper, its appeal to the intelligence, psychical, aesthetic, emotional power in the nature and its highest spiritual significance which leads through some one truth of the Godhead into the essence of spirituality. One may note too that in the practice of Yoga the disciple has to be led through his nature and according to his capacity and the spiritual teacher and guide is expected to perceive and take account of the necessary gradations and the individual need and power in his giving of help and guidance.

Many things may be objected to in the actual working of this large and flexible system and I shall take some note of them when I have to deal with the weak points or the pejorative side of the culture against which the hostile critic directs with a misleading exaggeration his missiles. But the principle of it and the main lines of the application embody a remarkable wisdom, knowledge and careful observation of human nature and an assured insight into the things of the spirit which none can question who has considered deeply and flexibly these difficult matters or had any close experience of the obstacles and potentialities of our nature in its approach to the concealed spiritual reality.

This carefully graded and complex system of religious development and spiritual evolution was linked on by a process of pervading intimate connection to that general culture of the life of the human being and his powers which must be the first care of every civilisation worth the name. The most delicate and difficult part of this task of human development is concerned with the thinking being of man, his mind of reason and knowledge. No ancient culture of which we have knowledge, not even the Greek, attached more importance to it or spent more effort on its cultivation. The business of the ancient Rishi was not only to know God, but to know the world and life and to reduce it by knowledge to a thing well understood and mastered with which the reason and will of man could deal on assured lines and on a safe basis of wise method and order. The ripe result of this effort was the Shastra. When we speak of the Shastra nowadays, we mean too often only the religiosocial system of injunctions of the middle age made sacrosanct by their mythical attribution to Manu, Parashara and other Vedic sages. But in older India Shastra meant any systematised teaching and science; each department of life, each line of activity, each subject of knowledge had its science or Shastra. The attempt was to reduce each to a theoretical and practical order founded on detailed observation, just generalisation, full experience, intuitive, logical experimental analysis and synthesis, in order to enable man know always with a just fruitfulness for life and to act with the security of right knowledge. The smallest and the greatest things were examined with equal care and attention and each provided with its art and science. The name was given even to the highest spiritual knowledge whenever it was stated not in a mass of intuitive experience and revelatory knowledge as in the Upanishads, but for intellectual comprehension in system and order,—and in that sense the Gita is able to call its profound spiritual teaching the most secret science, guhyatamam sastram. This high scientific and philosophical spirit was carried by the ancient Indian culture into all its activities. No Indian religion is complete without its outward form of preparatory practice, its supporting philosophy and its Yoga or system of inward practice or art of spiritual living: most even of what seems irrational in it to a first glance, has its philosophical turn and significance. It is this complete understanding and philosophical character which has given religion in India its durable security and immense vitality and enabled it to resist the acid dissolvent power of modern sceptical inquiry; whatever is illfounded in experience and reason, that power can dissolve, but not the heart and mind of these great teachings. But what we have more especially to observe is that while Indian culture made a distinction between the lower and the higher learning, the knowledge of things and the knowledge of self, it did not put a gulf between them like some religions, but considered the knowledge of the world and things as a preparatory and a leading up to the knowledge of Self and God. All Shastra was put under the sanction of the names of the Rishis, who were in the beginning the teachers not only of spiritual truth and philosophy,—and we may note that all Indian philosophy, even the logic of Nyaya and the atomic theory of the Vaisheshikas, has for its highest crowning note and eventual object spiritual knowledge and liberation,—but of the arts, the social, political and military, the physical and psychic sciences, and every instructor was in his degree respected as a guru or acarya, a guide or preceptor of the human spirit. All knowledge was woven into one and led up by degrees to the one highest knowledge.

The whole right practice of life founded on this knowledge was in the view of Indian culture a Dharma, a living according to a just understanding and right view of selfculture, of the knowledge of things and life and of action in that knowledge. Thus each man and class and kind and species and each activity of soul, mind, life, body has its Dharma. But the largest or at least most vitally important part of the Dharma was held to be the culture and ordering of the ethical nature of man. The ethical aspect of life, contrary to the amazingly ignorant observation of a certain type of critics, attracted a quite enormous amount of attention, occupied the greater part of Indian thought and writing not devoted to the things of pure knowledge and of the spirit and was so far pushed that there is no ethical formation or ideal which does not reach in it its highest conception and a certain divine absolutism of ideal practice. Indian thought took for granted,—though there are some remarkable speculations to the contrary, the ethical nature of man and the ethical law of the world. It considered that man was justified in satisfying his desires, since that is necessary for the satisfaction and expansion of life, but not in obeying the dictates of desire as the law of his being; for in all things there is a greater law, each has not only its side of interest and desire, but its dharma or rule of right practice, satisfaction, expansion, regulation. The Dharma, then, fixed by the wise in the Shastra is the right thing to observe, the true rule of action. First in the web of Dharma comes the social law; for man's life is only initially for his vital, personal, individual self but much more imperatively for the community, though most imperatively of all for the greatest Self one in himself and in all beings, for God, for the Spirit. Therefore first the individual must subordinate himself to the communal self, though by no means bound altogether to efface himself in it as the extremist of the communal idea imagine. He must live according to the law of his nature harmonised with the law of his social type and class, for the nation and in a higher reach of his being—this was greatly stressed by the Buddhists—for humanity. Thus living and acting he could learn to transcend the social scale of the Dharma, practise without injuring the basis of life the ideal scale and finally grow into the liberty of the spirit, when rule and duty were not binding because he would then move and act in a highest free and immortal dharma of the divine nature. All these aspects of the Dharma were closely linked up together in a progressive unity. Thus, for an example, each of the four orders had its own social function and ethics, but also an ideal rule for the growth of the pure ethical being, and every man by observing his dharma and turning his action Godwards could grow out of it into the spiritual freedom. But behind all dharma and ethics was put, not only as a safeguard but as a light, a religious sanction, a reminder of the continuity of life and of man's long pilgrimage through many births, a reminder of the Gods and planes beyond and of the Divine, and above it all the vision of a last stage of perfect comprehension and unity and of divine transcendence.

The system of Indian ethics liberalised by the catholicity of the ancient mind did not ban or violently discourage the aesthetic or even the hedonistic being of man in spite of a growing ascetic tendency and a certain high austerity of the summits. The aesthetic satisfactions of all kinds and all grades were an important part of the culture. Poetry, the drama, song, dance, music, the greater and lesser arts were placed under the sanction of the Rishis and were made instruments of the spirit's culture. A just theory held them to be initially the means of a pure aesthetic satisfaction and each was founded on its own basic rule and law, but on that basis and with a perfect fidelity to it still raised up to minister to the intellectual, ethical and religious development of the being. It is notable that the two vast Indian epics have been considered as much as Dharmashastras as great historicomythic epic narratives, itihasas. They are, that is to say, noble, vivid and puissant pictures of life, but they utter and breathe throughout their course the law and ideal of a great and high ethical and religious spirit in life and aim in their highest intention at the idea of the Divine and the way of the mounting soul in the action of the world. Indian painting, sculpture and architecture did not refuse service to the aesthetic satisfaction and interpretation of the social, civic and individual life of the human being; these things, as all evidences show, played a great part in their motives of creation, but still their highest work was reserved for the greatest spiritual side of the culture, and throughout we see them seized and suffused with the brooding stress of the Indian mind on the soul, the Godhead, the spiritual, the Infinite. And we have to note too that the aesthetic and hedonistic being was made not only an aid to religion and spirituality and liberally used for that purpose, but even one of the main gates of man's approach to the Spirit. The Vaishnava religion especially is a religion of love and beauty and of the satisfaction of the whole delight soul of man in God and even the desires and images of the sensuous life were turned by its vision into figures of a divine soul experience. Few religions have gone so far as this immense catholicity or carried the whole nature so high in its large, puissant and manysided approach to the spiritual and the infinite.

Finally, there is the most outwardly vital life of man, his ordinary dynamic, political, economical and social being. This too Indian culture took strenuously in hand and subjected its whole body to the pressure of its own ideals and conceptions. Its method was to build up great shastras of social living, duty and enjoyment, military and political rule and conduct and economical wellbeing. These were directed on one side to success, expansion, opulence and the right art and relation of these activities, but on those motives, demanded by the very nature of the vital man and his action, was imposed the law of the Dharma, a stringent social and ethical ideal and rule—thus the whole life of the king as the head of power and responsibility was regulated by it in its every hour and function,—and the constant reminder of religious duty. In latter times a Machiavellian principle of statecraft, that which has been always and is still pursued by governments and diplomats, encroached on this nobler system, but in the best age of Indian thought this depravation was condemned as a temporarily effective, but lesser, ignoble and inferior way of policy. The great rule of the culture was that the higher a man's position and power, the larger the scope of his function and influence of his acts and example, the greater should be the call on him of the Dharma. The whole law and custom of society was placed under the sanction of the Rishis and the gods, protected from the violence of the great and powerful, given a socioreligious character and the king himself charged to live and rule as the guardian and servant of the Dharma with only an executive power over the community which was valid so long as he observed with fidelity the Law. And as this vital aspect of life is the one which most easily draws us outward and away from the inner self and the diviner aim of living, it was the most strenuously linked up at every point with the religious idea in the way the vital man can best understand, in the Vedic times by the constant reminder of the sacrifice behind every social and civic act, at a later period by religious rites, ceremonies, worship, the calling in of the gods, the insistence on the subsequent results or a supraterrestrial aim of works. So great was this preoccupation, that while in the spiritual and intellectual and other spheres a considerable or a complete liberty was allowed to speculation, action, creation, here the tendency was to impose a rigorous law and authority, a tendency which in the end became greatly exaggerated and prevented the expansion of the society into new forms more suitable for the need of the spirit of the age, the Yugadharma. A door of liberty was opened to the community by the provision of an automatic permission to change custom and to the individual in the adoption of the religious life with its own higher discipline or freedom outside the ordinary social weft of binding rule and injunction. A rigid observation and discipline of the social law, a larger nobler discipline and freer selfculture of the ideal side of the Dharma, a wide freedom of the religious and spiritual life became the three powers of the system. The steps of the expanding human spirit mounted through these powers to its perfection.

Thus the whole general character of the application of Indian ideals to life became throughout of this one texture, the constant, subtly graded, subtly harmonised preparation of the soul of man for its spiritual being. First, the regulated satisfaction of the primary natural being of man subjected to the law of the Dharma and the ethical idea and besieged at every moment by the suggestions of religion, a religion at first appealing to his more outward undeveloped mind, but in each of its outward symbols and circumstances opening to a profounder significance, armed with the indication of a profoundest spiritual and ideal meaning as its justification. Then, the higher steps of the developed reason and psychical, ethical and aesthetic powers closely interwoven and raised by a similar opening beyond themselves to their own heights of spiritual direction and potentiality. Finally, each of these growing powers in man was made on its own line of approach a gateway into his divine and spiritual being. Thus we may observe that there was created a Yoga of knowledge for the selfexceeding of the thinking intellectual man, a Yoga of works for the selfexceeding of the active, dynamic and ethical man, a Yoga of love and bhakti for the selfexceeding of the emotional, aesthetic, hedonistic man, by which each arrived to perfection through a selfward, spiritual, Godward direction of his own special power, as too a Yoga of selfexceeding through the power of the psychical being and even through the power of the life in the body, —Yogas which could be practised in separation or with some kind of synthesis. But all these ways of selfexceeding led to a highest selfbecoming. To become one with universal being and all existences, one with the self and spirit, united with God completed the human evolution, built the final step of man's selfculture.

...A nation is building in India today before the eyes of the world so swiftly, so palpably that all can watch the process and those who have sympathy and intuition distinguish the forces at work, the materials in use, the lines of the divine architecture. This nation is not a new race raw from the workshop of Nature or created by modern circumstances. One of the oldest races and greatest civilisations on this earth, the most Indomitable in vitality, the most fecund in greatness, the deepest in life, the most wonderful in potentiality, after taking into itself numerous sources of strength from foreign strains of blood and other types of human civilisation, is now seeking to lift itself for good into an organised national unity. Formerly a congeries of kindred nations with a single life and a single culture, always by the law of this essential oneness tending to unity, always by its excess of fecundity engendering fresh diversities and divisions, it has never yet been able to overcome permanently the almost insuperable obstacles to the organisation of a continent. The time has now come when those obstacles can be overcome. The attempt which our race has been making throughout its long history, it will now make under entirely new circumstances. We believe that it is sure to succeed because the freedom, unity and greatness of India have now become necessary to the world. We believe that God is with us and in that faith we shall conquer. We believe that humanity needs us and it is the love and service of humanity, of our country, of the race, of our religion that will purify our heart and inspire our action in the struggle.

The task we set before ourselves is not mechanical but moral and spiritual. We aim not at the alteration of a form of government but at the building up of a nation. Of that task politics is a part, but only a part. We shall devote ourselves not to politics alone, nor to social questions alone, nor to theology or philosophy or literature or science by themselves, but we include all these in one entity which we believe to be all important, the *dharma*. the national religion which we also believe to be universal. There is a mighty law of life, a great principle of human evolution, a body of spiritual knowledge and experience of which India has always been destined to be guardian, exemplar and missionary. This is the *sanatana dharma,* the eternal religion. Under the stress of alien impacts she has largely lost hold not of the structure of that *dharma,* but of its living reality. For the religion of India is nothing if it is not lived. It has to be applied not only to life, but to the whole of life; its spirit has to enter into and mould our society, our politics, our literature, our science, our individual character, affections and aspirations. To understand the heart of this *dharma,* to experience it as a truth, to feel the high emotions to which it rises and to express and execute it in life is what we understand by Karmayoga. We believe that it is to make the yoga the ideal of human life that India rises today; by the yoga she will get the strength to realise her freedom, unity and greatness, by the yoga she will keep the strength to preserve it. It is a spiritual revolution we foresee and the material is only its shadow and reflex.

We believe that India is destined to work out her own independent life and civilisation, to stand in the forefront of the world and solve the political, social, economic and moral problems which Europe has failed to solve, yet the pursuit of which and the feverish passage in that pursuit from experiment to experiment, from failure to failure she calls her progress. Our means must be as great as our ends and the strength to discover and use the means so as to attain the end can only be found by seeking the eternal source of strength in ourselves.

We do not believe that by multiplying new sects limited within the narrower and inferior ideas of religion imported from the West or by creating organisations for the perpetuation of the mere dress and body of Hinduism we can recover our spiritual health, energy and greatness. The world moves through an indispensable interregnum of free thought and materialism to a new synthesis of religious thought and experience, a new religious world life free from intolerance, yet full of faith and fervour, accepting all forms of religion because it has an unshakable faith in the One. The religion which embraces Science and faith, Theism, Christianity, Mahomedanism and Buddhism and yet is none of these, is that to which the World Spirit moves. In our own, which is the most sceptical and the most believing of all, the most sceptical because it has questioned and experimented the most, the most believing because it has the deepest experience and the most varied and positive spiritual knowledge, —that wider Hinduism which is not a dogma or combination of dogmas but a law of life, which is not a social framework but the spirit of a past and future social evolution, which rejects nothing but insists on testing and experiencing everything and when tested and experienced, turning it to the soul's uses, in this Hinduism we find the basis of the future world religion. This *sanatana dharma* has many scriptures, Veda, Vedanta, Gita, Upanishad, Darshana, Purana, Tantra, nor could it reject the Bible or the Koran; but its real, most authoritative scripture is in the heart in which the Eternal has His dwelling. It is in our inner spiritual experiences that we shall find the proof and source of the world's Scriptures, the law of knowledge, love and conduct, the basis and inspiration of Karmayoga.

Our aim will therefore be to help in building up India for the sake of humanity. We say to humanity: "The time has come when you must take the great step and rise out of a material existence into the higher, deeper and wider life towards which humanity moves. The problems which have troubled mankind can only be solved by conquering the kingdom within, not by harnessing the forces of Nature to the service of comfort and luxury, but by mastering the forces of the intellect and the spirit, by vindicating the freedom of man within as well as without and by conquering from within external Nature. For that work the resurgence of Asia is necessary, therefore Asia rises..."

We say to the nation: "It is God's will that we should be ourselves and not Europe. We have sought to regain life by following the law of another being than our own. We must return and seek the sources of life and strength within ourselves. We must know our past and recover it for the purposes of our future. Our business is to realise ourselves first and to mould everything to the law of India's eternal life and nature... [We must] read the heart of our religion, our society, our philosophy, politics, literature, art. jurisprudence, science, thought, everything that was and is ours, so that we may be able to say to ourselves and our nation, This is our *dharma*. We shall review European civilisation entirely from the standpoint of Indian thought and knowledge and seek to throw off from us the dominating stamp of the Occident; what we have to take from the West we shall take as Indians. And the *dharma* once discovered, we shall strive our utmost not only to profess but to live, in our individual actions, in our Social life, in our political endeavours."

We say to the individual and especially to the young who are now arising to do India's work, the world's work. God's work: "You cannot cherish these ideals, still less can you fulfil them if you subject your minds to European ideas or look at life from the material standpoint. Materially you are nothing, spiritually you are everything. It is only the Indian who can believe everything, dare everything, sacrifice everything. First, therefore, become

Indians. Recover the patrimony of your forefathers. Recover the Aryan thought, the Aryan discipline, the Aryan character, the Aryan life. Recover the Vedanta the Gita, the Yoga. Recover them not only in intellect or sentiment but in your lives. Live them and you will be great and strong, mighty, invincible and fearless. Neither life nor death will have any terrors for you. Difficulty and impossibility will vanish from your vocabularies. For it is in the spirit that strength is eternal and you must win back the kingdom of yourselves, the inner Swaraj, before you can win back your outer empire. There the Mother dwells and She waits for worship that She may give strength. Believe in Her, serve Her, lose your wills in Hers, your egoism in the greater ego of the country, your separate selfishness in the service of humanity. Recover the source of all strength in yourselves and all else will be added to you. social soundness, intellectual preeminence, political freedom, the mastery of human thought. the hegemony of the world."

...The need of a great ideal was never more keenly felt than it is in India at the present day. Nowhere have so many weaknesses combined to stand in the way of a nation in the whole range of history...

What strength will help her to shake off the weaknesses which have crowded in on her? How will she raise herself from the dust whom a thousand shackles bind down? Only the strength of a superhuman ideal, only the gigantic force of a superhuman will, only the vehemence of an effort which transcends all that man has done and approaches divinity. Where will she find that strength, that force, that vehemence? In herself.

India has in herself a faith of superhuman virtue to accomplish miracles, to deliver herself out of irrefragable bondage, to bring God down upon earth. She has a secret of will power which no other nation possesses. All she needs to rouse in her that faith, that will, is an ideal which will induce her to make the effort. The ideal is that of humanity in God, of God in humanity, the ancient ideal of the *sanatana dharma* but applied, as it has never been applied before, to the problem of politics and the: work of national revival. To realise that ideal, to impart it to the world is the nation of India. She has evolved a religion which embraces all that the heart, the brain, the practical faculty of man can desire but she has not yet applied it to the problems of modern politics. This therefore is the work which she has still to do before she can help humanity; the necessity of the mission is the justification for her resurgence, the great incentive of saving herself to save mankind is the native power which will give her the force, the strength, the vehemence which can alone enable her to realise her destiny. No lesser ideal will help her...

We are Hindus and naturally spiritual in our temperament, because the work which we have to do for humanity is a work which no other nation can accomplish, the spiritualisation of the race. When scepticism had reached its height, the time had come for spirituality to assert itself and establish the reality of the world as a manifestation of the spirit, the secret of the confusion created by the senses, the magnificent possibilities of man and the ineffable beatitude of God.

Mankind has long been experimenting with various kinds of thought, different principles of ethics, strange dreams of a perfection to be gained by material means, impossible millenniums and humanitarian hopes. Nowhere has it succeeded in realising the ultimate secret of life. Nowhere has it found satisfaction. No scheme of society or politics has helped it to escape from the necessity of sorrow, poverty, strife, dissatisfaction from which it strives for an outlet; for whoever is trying to find one by material means must inevitably fail. The East alone has some knowledge of the truth, the East alone can teach the West, the East alone can save mankind. Through all these ages Asia has been seeking for a light within, and whenever she has been blessed with a glimpse of what she seeks, a great religion has been born. Buddhism, Confucianism, Christianity, Mahomedanism with all their countless sects. But the grand workshop of spiritual experiment, the laboratory of the soul has been India, where thousands of great spirits have been born in every generation who were content to work quietly in their own souls, perfect their knowledge, hand down the results of their experiments to a few disciples and leave the rest to others to complete. They did not hasten to proselytise, were in no way eager to proclaim themselves, but merely added their quota of experience and returned to the source from which they had come. The immense reservoir of spiritual energy stored up by the selfrepression was the condition of this birth of *avataras,* of men so full of God that they could not be satisfied with silent bliss, but poured it out on the world, not with the idea of proselytising but because they wished to communicate their own ecstasy of realisation to others who were fit to receive it either by previous tapasya or by the purity of their desires. Of all these souls Sri Ramakrishna was the last and greatest, for while others felt God in a single or limited aspect, he felt Him in His illimitable unity as the sum of an illimitable variety. In him the spiritual experiences of the millions of saints who had gone before were renewed and united. Sri Ramakrishna gave to India the final message of Hinduism to the world. A new era dates from his birth, an era in which the peoples of the earth will be lifted for a while into communion with God and spirituality become the dominant note of human life. What Christianity failed to do, what Mahomedanism strove to accomplish in times as yet unripe, what Buddhism half accomplished for a brief period and among a limited number of men, Hinduism as summed up in the life of Sri Ramakrishna has to attempt for all the world...The movement of which the first outbreak was political, will end in a spiritual consummation.

Index